Shazi Zaman is a graduate in History from St. Stephen's College, Delhi. He started his three and a half decade long career in electronic media at Doordarshan in 1988 and has since then worked with several media organizations like BBC World Service, Aaj Tak, Zee News and Star News. Shaping news channels has been his vocation and also an area of interest. He has served as the Group Editor of the ABP News Network and also Director, Video Services of the Press Trust of India. He has been on the governing bodies of the Film and Television Institute of India, Pune, and the Indian Institute of Mass Communication, Delhi. His Hindi novels include *Prem Gali Ati Sankri*, *Jism Jism ke Log* and *Akbar*, which he also translated into English. He has also authored a book for children, *The Alligator and the Stapler and Other Magical Tales*.

AKBAR

The Great CEO

The Emperor's 30 Rules of Leadership

Shazi Zaman

SPEAKING
TIGER

SPEAKING TIGER BOOKS LLP
125A, Ground Floor, Shahpur Jat, near Asiad Village,
New Delhi 110049

First published by Speaking Tiger in 2024

ISBN: 978-93-5447-888-8
eISBN: 978-93-5447-990-8

10 9 8 7 6 5 4 3 2 1

Typeset in Adobe Jenson Pro by SÜRYA, New Delhi
Printed at HT Media Ltd, Greater Noida

In memory of my friend Asif,
who lived like a king

And indeed he was a great king; for he knew that the good ruler is one who can command simultaneously, the obedience, the respect, the love, and the fear of his subjects. He was a prince beloved of all, firm with the great, kind to those of low estate, and just to all men, high and low, neighbour or stranger, Christian, Saracen, or Gentile; so that every man believed that the King was on his side.

—A Jesuit priest stationed at Akbar's court

Contents

Preface

The Mughal throne was for life. Mughal Emperors did not ascend the throne intending to retire at some point. They believed they would rule in perpetuity. Their entire kingly career was geared towards this end. But despite the story of invincibility that was woven around the Emperors, they knew that they were vulnerable and that they had to perform, defend, consolidate and expand to safeguard themselves and ensure obedience, compliance and loyalty.

While the primary aim of all Emperors—and Akbar was no different—was to perpetuate their rule and remove, by the most effective means, anything that stood in their way, Akbar was too shrewd and wise a ruler to say so bluntly. His official spokesperson Abul Fazl created a big picture—and a larger purpose—for the empire: that it existed to bring more and more people under *zil-i-Ilahi*, Jalaluddin Muhammad Akbar's umbrella of justice. The Emperor thus had a story which justified his right to rule.

He also perfected the art of ruling with a light touch even though he had the means to be brutal. In an age when asserting control over an expanding empire was of paramount importance, Akbar cultivated various habits which allowed him to rule through subtler tactics than many of his forebears and contemporaries.

As I read the *Akbarnama*—the tome Akbar commissioned to give permanence to his life and message—and looked at the grand paintings and monuments he commissioned, it struck me that one can identify with the practical wisdom that enabled him to be at the top for half a century. Times may change but a lot remains the same under the surface. There are some practices that were specific to Akbar's time but behind the specifics there is a lot that is common to all times. The basic impulses that govern human beings (rulers and ruled alike) do not change even though you might be wearing a suit instead of a Mughal *jama*. This in sum is the story of this book—Emperor Akbar's 30 rules that every CEO should know.

Shazi Zaman

1

The Intrepid Leader

Let us two come into the field of battle and fight with one another with all the arms that he knows, so that whoever by divine decree, and the help of heaven, shall be the conqueror shall have the kingdom.

—Akbar inviting the self-styled Afghan king Daud Khan Karrani to personal combat

In 1574 CE, the powerful Emperor Jalaluddin Muhammad Akbar reached the outskirts of Patna where the self-styled Afghan king Daud Khan Karrani held the fort. Akbar's most trusted *mansabdar* Munim Khan, stationed outside Patna, had failed to defeat Daud Khan Karrani and neither had he been able to convince him to join the imperial service. The unexpected arrival of the Emperor at the height of the rainy season unnerved Daud Khan Karrani, who sent the following message to Akbar: "I do not approve for myself the title of sovereign...now obedience to the Emperor had taken possession of this heart. Whatever fief is given, I would consider it a piece of good fortune. Owing to youth and lack of wisdom, I have committed faults. So I would not kiss the threshold until I make amends by my service."

Under pressure, Daud Khan Karrani gave up his kingly ambitions but did not agree to be physically present at the royal court. Not convinced about the sincerity of Daud Khan's offer, Akbar decided that the case needed a final resolution. So he decided to confront him head on. He sent Daud a message: "We, by virtue of our being *zil-i-Ilahi*, receive little and give much. Our forgiveness has no relish for vengeance, provided that Daud has light from the torch of truth, and will rub his forehead on the threshold of fortune, so the hand of our grace may disperse the dust of destruction from the crown of his fortune. Otherwise let him do one of three things so that the lives and goods of so many thousands may not be an offering to ruin. First, let someone from his party come to our camp and be a spectator, and someone from our side go to his army and be a sentinel, so that no one on either side engages in war, and let us two come into the field of battle and fight with one another with all the arms that he knows, so that whoever by divine decree, and the help of heaven, shall be the conqueror shall have the kingdom. If his courage be not equal to this, let him choose someone of his soldiers who is distinguished for valour and strength of arm, and skill in combat. We shall also send one of our strong-armed ones, whose countenance shall be decked with might, against him. These two combatants will contend in the arena. The army of whichever of them conquers shall be victorious. If in his army there be no such lion-heart, then let him choose one of his host of elephants, and we too shall produce an elephant as majestic as heaven. Victory shall be on the side of whichever of them prevails."

An unnerved Daud Khan Karrani did not take up any of the three offers made by the Mughal Emperor. The Mughal forces launched a nocturnal amphibious attack on Hajipur, from where supplies were being sent to Patna. After Hajipur was captured, heads of Afghan warriors were arranged in a boat and sent to Daud Khan Karrani, who fled Patna in a drunken state. Soon afterwards he was killed and his head presented to Akbar.

This is one of the many examples in his career when Akbar decided that the time of negotiation was past and that he needed to lead from the front, even potentially putting his life at risk. When the Rubicon was to be crossed was a call that he took in a manner so unpredictable that his opponents could never gain an advantage by guessing it.

The Emperor's audacity was well documented visually as well, to remind those who had not seen it in person. In one painting he is seen holding a cheetah by its ear and in another painting he is seen mounted on a mast elephant and chasing another across a shaky bridge built on boats.

~

In consolidating and expanding his empire and spreading his influence far and wide, he excelled in being a step ahead of those who could oppose him. He himself appeared at the doorstep of his enemies when they least expected it. This unpredictability served him well.

Here comes the army of the mighty Emperor Akbar,
Subjects and kings of the seven islands and eight
directions tremble with fear.
Such is his speed that day and night have turned
into moments,

Jalaluddin Muhammad's army moves as if victory is
its second nature.
Shah Humayun's son is like sandalwood and sword,
Tansen submits that valuables be given him to ward
off the evil eye.

—Tansen, Akbar's courtier and
favourite singer-composer

2

Even the Truth Has to Await its Moment

In conquering and administering kingdoms, some things may appear appropriate and logical on the surface, but one has to consider a hundred thousand things behind every step.

—From the *Baburnama,* the autobiography of Akbar's grandfather Zahiruddin Muhammad Babur, which was often read out to the Emperor

It was very early in the reign of Jalaluddin Muhammad Akbar. He had just about gained control over most factions but, as would soon be revealed, there were many around who wanted him dead.

Akbar was in Delhi. He had just finished a hunt, offered prayers at the shrine of Nizamuddin Awliya and had reached a busy intersection (where even now there is a traffic light opposite the Old Fort) near the building called "Khairul Manazil"—a *madrasa* and a mosque built by Maham Anga. She had been Akbar's wet nurse and was once a prominent power behind the throne. But she and her headstrong son Adham Khan, who had invited Akbar's wrath by killing the Emperor's foster father, had been dead for some time.

It seems there was disquiet in the city over the Emperor's decision to marry into prominent families. Interestingly, this issue too was linked to Maham Anga's clan. Fatima, the widowed daughter-in-law of Sheikh Buddh, a notable person of Agra, entered into a relationship with Baqi Khan, who was the elder brother of Adham Khan and another son of Maham Anga. The relationship turned into a matrimonial alliance. The lady began taking another daughter-in-law of Sheikh Buddh to marriage ceremonies and other gatherings. That daughter-in-law was very beautiful and was married to a man called Abdul Wasi. When Emperor Akbar chanced upon her on some occasion, he sent a marriage proposal for her. Mongol law dictated that it was obligatory upon a man to divorce his wife if the Emperor took a fancy to her. So Abdul Wasi pronounced *talaq* thrice and left for the Deccan with the comment, "God's earth is wide."

Now Fatima began to instigate the Emperor, at the behest of Sheikh Buddh. She said that the Emperor should marry into other prominent families of Delhi and Agra so that all felt equal in his eyes. Thus when the Emperor reached Delhi, he expressed a desire to forge matrimonial relations with prominent families of the city. Middlemen and eunuchs were sent to prominent families to look for maidens but before any headway could be made an unforeseen event took place.

The Emperor was on horseback, and attended by a retinue. The usual regal paraphernalia of *saiban*—the parasol under which all subjects were to symbolically live in peace—was held above his head by an attendant. Just as he neared the busy intersection near the *madrasa* of Maham Anga, an arrow struck him near the shoulder. The shot had been fired from atop the *madrasa* by the slave of a man married to Akbar's step-sister. Whether the disaffected families of Delhi, who were unwilling to marry their daughters to the Emperor were behind this outrage or it was related to something else will never be known. The Emperor in his wisdom disallowed the interrogation of the assailant. He said, "Don't ask! God knows what all this slave would say and which loyalists would fall under suspicion. Don't let him speak. Finish him off."

Very clearly, the young Emperor—all of 21 years of age—was aware of threats from those close to him but thought that if the names were revealed, it would draw him into a direct confrontation with those accused. Perhaps he thought the time was not yet ripe for it. There are other instances where he waited years for the right time and then delivered the punishment he deemed fit. And of course there were, more often, times when he dealt exemplary punishment on the spot.

~

That the Emperor could spring a surprise by not revealing the truth gave him an advantage over his foes. It kept them in the dark about how much the Emperor knew. And it gave the Emperor room to manoeuvre, to take action when he was ready and strong enough to do so.

> *In the reciprocity of rule and obedience, the sanctions of hope and fear are necessary to the well-ordering of temporal government and the illumination of interior recesses of the spirit; nevertheless a masterful will, never suffering the loss of self-control under the dominance of passion, should weigh well and wisely the measure and occasion of each.*
>
> —Jalaluddin Muhammad Akbar in the *Ain-i-Akbari*, originally the last part of the *Akbarnama*

3

Lightning Response

The moon-like march of the Emperor's conveyance
was covering with dust even the shining sun:
The messenger of your fame is travelling across the
world,
Not allowing even doubt to accompany you.

—Arif Qandhari in the *Tarikh-i-Akbari,* the first chronicle of Akbar's reign, about Akbar's lightening nine-day march from Sikri to Ahmedabad

The prosperous province of Gujarat was Akbar's prize conquest. But soon after he reached Sikri after capturing Gujarat he got the disturbing news that the province was about to fall to Muhammad Hussain Mirza and Ibrahim Hussain Mirza who, like Akbar, were descendants of Amir Timur. The governor appointed by Akbar in Gujarat, Mirza Aziz Koka, was besieged in Ahmedabad. While the rich coastal province was of immense value to the empire, the governor Mirza Aziz Koka was especially dear to the Emperor. His mother Jiji Anga was one of the ladies who had breastfed Akbar. Akbar was fond of saying, "We and Mirza Aziz Koka are joined by a stream of milk." Weeping profusely, Jiji Anga told Akbar, "Do whatever you must. I want to see my son's face."

Akbar immediately dispatched the royal harem and thousands of soldiers and said, "They are going ahead of me but will reach after me."

Raja Bharmal, Raja Todar Mal and many trusted nobles were entrusted with the security of Fatehpur and Kunwar Man Singh was ordered to join the Emperor with the Kachhwaha Rajputs.

On Sunday the twenty-third of August, 1573 CE,

Jalaluddin Muhammad Akbar, accompanied by three hundred people, mounted a she-camel and set out on the swiftest journey of his career.

As predicted, on the way the entourage met the forces that had been sent in advance and overtook many of them, reaching the destination in record time. Abul Fazl wrote: "To make a long story short, the world's lord being possessed of a right intention, an upright mind, supreme confidence in God, and a lofty courage, and also because by giving even small attention to the matter, 300 or 400 first-rate troopers could be collected in a short space of time, accomplished in nine days such a long journey—which caravans took two or three months to effect."

When the rebel Muhammad Hussain Mirza saw Jalaluddin Muhammad Akbar's army on the other side of the Sabarmati, he shouted and asked, "Whose army is this?"

A soldier replied, "This is Badshah Salamat's army that has come to teach a lesson to the disloyal."

Muhammad Hussain Mirza said, "My men left Fatehpur fourteen days ago. If this is the royal army, where are the royal elephants who are never separate from the royal army?"

The soldier replied, "How would elephants mighty as the mountain travel with the army and cover four hundred *kos* in nine days?"

Although some in the army felt that they should wait for reinforcements because the enemy was far superior in numbers, Emperor Akbar said, "In all enterprises and especially in this expedition all my reliance is on Divine aid. If I had looked to ordinary means I ought not to have come this long journey so unattended."

With this he plunged into the swollen river and his army followed him. In the fierce battle that took place, Muhammad Hussain Mirza was captured.

With the battle won, Emperor Akbar's foster brother Mirza Aziz Koka was rescued and the head of Muhammad Hussain Mirza was dispatched to Fatehpur and Agra for public display.

~

Despite numerical inferiority, it was the element of extreme speed and surprise that won the battle. But for Akbar each challenge deserved a different strategy because he was not predictable. Predictable action would make him vulnerable. His foes were kept in suspense about what strategy he would pursue—long rope or lightning march.

The chariot goes as swift as a cloud,
Like as patience departs from lovers,
From the rapid going outside and inside
The echo reaches the skies.

—Sheikh Abul Fazl about the swift march from Sikri to Ahmedabad

4

Never Do the Obvious

The king should keep his secrets concealed, so that he can change his mind without sounding contradictory. This is also necessary for the reason that the enemy would become vigilant if he gets to know the plans. The need to keep secrets has to be combined with the need to consult intelligent people. This is possible by only consulting men who are intelligent and have administrative abilities and who would not publicize their opinion...When a matter has been decided, one should mix the first steps in the desired direction with steps opposite to it. One should not go to extremes in either direction because it might evoke suspicion or give away the actual plan.

—From the *Akhlaq-i-Nasiri,* a 13th-century text on etiquette and way of life; it was one of Akbar's favourite books which he also recommended to his officers

In the month of May in 1578, twenty-three years into his reign, an Emperor who was very confident of himself did something that took everyone by surprise. For days a massive preparation was on for a great hunt—*qamargah* as it was called—around Bhera in Punjab. No less than fifty thousand soldiers had laid siege and over several days closed in so that the animals were finally hemmed into a small area with no scope of escape, and the Emperor and the imperial entourage could hunt them with ease. However, shortly before the great game was to commence, Akbar apparently went into a trance and called off the hunt. Contemporary watchers saw the decision as impelled by His Majesty's mystical urges. However, the fact was that the hunt was actually a war game conducted not far from the fief of his recalcitrant half-brother Mirza Hakim who ruled from Kabul. With the objective of a show of strength achieved, the killing of animals had become incidental.

If one takes a look at the route he took to travel from Ajmer to Bhera, one is struck by the fact that he deliberately took a longer route. Taking unexpected turns at many places, he stopped at shrines to offer prayers and completely bypassed Lahore. Anybody tracking the route would have been confused about the motives of Emperor Akbar. In taking an indirect path he might have thrown Mirza Hakim off his scent.

Whether it was the appearance of Akbar's mother Hamida Banu Begum on the scene that averted a direct confrontation between the half-brothers or that Akbar thought that the time for the military option was not yet ripe, Akbar decided to go no farther than delivering a warning through his presence with his fifty thousand men. As subsequent years would reveal, military action was merely deferred, not given up.

For now, having sent a stern message across, he suddenly decided to give diplomacy a chance. In the words of the Emperor: "My sole wish is that the Mirza may emerge from the defile of savagery and be encompassed with princely favours. Inasmuch as he is young and inexperienced, and is associated with persons of small capacity, perchance he may on our approach turn away from the altar of fortune and go and take refuge with Uzbeks. Though able and farsighted men have regarded a younger brother in the light of a son, yet something tells me that the existence of a dutiful son is doubtful, and the meeting of brothers impossible. It is far better that I hearten him with good counsel from a distance. It may be that his somnolent fortune shall awake and that he shall take the path of obedience, cease to stray, and become a traveller to the abode of bliss. If under the influence of the evil ones he has hurried away from the high road of obedience and the pleasant abode of service, and has fallen into the thornbrake of ingratitude, it becomes a magnanimous nature to act contrary to the nature of the short-sighted."

This incident is a classic case of not doing the obvious, whether it was in the route he took, or the war game he played and called off, seemingly at a momentary impulse. This is a stratagem he used to good effect many a time in his life. Of course, this further reinforced the aura that was built around him—of him being far-seeing and all-seeing, and of being able to see what none could.

There was ambiguity about where he stood in other contexts as well. The Jesuit Father Acquaviva wrote in a letter, "People here have various views about the King. Some believe he is a Christian, others that he is a Hindu, and others a Muslim. Some other people with better judgement think he is neither a Christian, nor a Hindu, nor a Muslim. In my view this is true, or perhaps he is a Muslim, but conforms to all to win the goodwill of all."

~

It must have been psychologically unsettling for any foe or challenger to find Akbar not doing the obvious. This definitely gave a clear edge to His Majesty many times in his kingly career and kept him on top of the game.

Whenever he went out hunting with his hunters, it not only created hysteria in the hearts and minds of his companions, but unleashed a wave of terror among all beasts and birds of that region. So much so if birds had heard the news of his approach, they would have drowned themselves like ducks with sheer fright if they had the power.

—Muhammad Arif Qandhari in the *Tarikh-i-Akbari,*
the first chronicle of Akbar's reign

5

No Option But To Grow

March, march, march away
March for you will be victorious.

—a verse composed for Emperor Akbar
when he was contemplating the Deccan
expedition and asked for an augury

The Mughal empire in its healthy days was constantly expanding. In fact, expansion was built into the working of the empire. The *mansabdari* system was the mechanism that ensured the recruitment and nurturing of the best available talent to run and expand the empire. From what Akbar inherited when Humayun died to what he left at his death after half a century of rule and expansion, the map of the empire had rapidly changed to include territories that now lie in four countries.

It was left to Abul Fazl—His Majesty's most eloquent spokesperson—to rationalize that the expanding the empire was all about spreading justice and freeing people from tyranny.

However, the plain fact was that territorial expansion had the potential of yielding rich territories, making the empire richer and ever more formidable. And expansion was the best antidote to contraction. Akbar himself put it very clearly, in the *Ain-i-Akbari,* of course without taking names, "A monarch should be ever intent on conquest. Otherwise his neighbours rise in arms against him. The army should be exercised in warfare, lest from want of training they become self-indulgent."

Akbar's expansionism sent a message to his powerful

neighbours—Iran, Turan and the Ottoman empire—that the Emperor of Hindustan was not one to be trifled with. Thus the polite mention by Emperor Akbar of his imperial successes in the letter to Abdullah Khan Uzbek, the ruler of Turan—"...conquest of a vast country like Hindustan which was surrounded by the ocean on three sides and has been described by travellers as a very big country—even calling it fourth-sixth part of the world—was not actually meant to fulfil my own ambition but to protect the oppressed."

Likewise the invitation to the Jesuits was meant as much to understand their faith as well as to know more about the Portuguese power that had reached the vicinity of the Mughal empire. One can imagine that Akbar also wanted them to see at first hand the dazzle and might of his empire.

This posturing—as well as the threat that lay behind it—did not escape the Jesuits at Akbar's court. Father Acquaviva wrote to the Superior General of the Society of Jesus, "We have no idea whether he is a friend or an enemy of the King of Portugal but we have noticed some things we do not like. He has ambitions to be the greatest king of all, and apparently he cannot tolerate that the King of Portugal be the lord of the sea, and that his own ships have to pay taxes in the ports of the King of Portugal."

~

Bringing more and more territories and people under the imperial umbrella was a task that constantly occupied Akbar. It kept his foes at bay and made the empire stronger. It enhanced his stature within and outside the empire and lent further strength to his aura of invincibility. In sum, expansion was the growth story the Emperor could not do without.

Kashi, Kashmir, Kamru, Karnatak, Bundi,
Bundelkhand,
Malwa, Multan, Mewar, Khurasan, Balkh, Bukhara,
Gokulmand,
Bijapur, Bang, Badakhshan, Rum, Siam and Bharat,
Says Tansen, the universe fears Humayun's son
Jalaluddin Akbar.

—Tansen, the celebrated
poet-singer of Akbar's court

6

Loyalty—The Two-way Street

"[I was caught by] Badshah Salamat's salt."

—reply of the rebel Muhammad Hussain Mirza
when asked who caught him on the battlefield

At a time when power was often won and retained on the basis of personal performance, the Emperor and his men had to win each other's support on a continuous basis. The Emperor's charisma had to be matched by actual performance to win people's loyalty. On various critical occasions the Emperor took a stand that was outrageous and risky but won the admiration and support of his men.

The blitzkrieg that took Akbar from Sikri to Gujarat in nine days was meant to surprise and chastise the rebels, but there was one more reason behind this urgency. His foster brother Mirza Aziz Koka, with whom he was "linked by a stream of milk," as the Emperor himself put it, was under siege in the city of Ahmedabad.

When the army was assembled for inspection near Ahmedabad, the Emperor discovered that Rupsi's son Jaimal, the nephew of Raja Bharmal of Amber, had ill-fitting armour. The Emperor gave him a new set, and Jaimal's old armour was given to Karan, the grandson of Raja Maldeo of Jodhpur. When Rupsi discovered that his family armour had been given to a member of the royal house of Jodhpur, he asked the Emperor for it to be returned. He was so offended that, despite Akbar's efforts to mollify him, Rupsi took off his own armour and decided to go into the battlefield without it. At this juncture when the army was getting ready for a crucial battle near Ahmedabad, Akbar said, "Our brave men would fight without armour! So it will not agree with valour that we should go armed into the battlefield. We shall also face the arrows and swords like this."

Raja Bhagwant Das, the son of Raja Bharmal of Amber, then raced his horse and came up to Rupsi. He counselled him to relent and defused the situation.

Shortly afterwards, in the course of this battle a person was brought in as a prisoner who had killed Bhagwant Das' brother Bhupat in the Battle of Sarnal during Akbar's previous military campaign in Gujarat. Bhupat lost his life fighting as his forces were outnumbered. The Emperor had close matrimonial ties with the royal house of Amber to which Bhupat and his brother Bhagwant Das belonged. He had sent his wife, the sister of Bhupat, to be present for mourning at Amber. Now, presented with the killer of Bhupat, he raised his spear and killed him.

It was his policy to stand for those who stood for him. During the course of an elephant fight, staged for entertainment, one of the beasts suddenly turned towards Raja Birbal. To save Birbal's life the Emperor sped on his horse and obstructed the elephant's path. Years later, when Raja Birbal lost his life fighting the Yusufzai rebels, the Emperor was so grief stricken that he abstained from his official duties—one of the very few occasions when he did so. He wrote to Abdur Rahim Khan-i-Khanan: "Raja Birbal was among the closest of the close—a faithful, sincere, wise and knowledgeable courtier, a companion of pleasant gatherings, a loyalist, a well-wisher, a person who shone in the gathering of fluent orators, one who had an insight into human associations, a relentless seeker of truth, a person with firm belief in discharging obligations, a good-natured son, truly a devoted person, and a jewel of the sacred abode of sovereignty. Despite being in the worldly state of bondage, he had been free. Having now sacrificed his life for the Emperor, he has departed from this ephemeral world and taken a path which all must take. Even the obligation of surrendering life for the master was fulfilled while discharging his imperial duties...Although our feelings for him are known to those close to us, we wish to express it fully so that everybody realizes how the Emperor values the devoted ones."

That Raja Birbal's body could not be found remained a cause of deep sorrow to the Emperor. He lamented, "Alas, that they could not bring his body out of that defile, that it might have been consigned to the flames."

When Tansen died, Akbar ordered his musicians and singers to accompany the body on its last journey. He said, "Tansen's death is the annihilation of music."

Akbar's attachment to his loyalists is evident from his acute pain and grief at their departure from this world. He visited Abul Faiz Faizi—Abul Fazl's brother—on his death bed, caressed his head and said, "Sheikh Ji, I have brought Hakim Ali with me. Will you not speak to me?" Getting no reply, the Emperor threw his turban on the ground and wept loudly. Then he consoled Sheikh Abul Fazl and left.

When Prince Salim had Abul Fazl killed because he thought that the Sheikh was a stumbling block to his kingly ambitions, and the head was dispatched to the prince, the Emperor was grief stricken and did not see anybody for many days. He said, "If Salim wished to be the Emperor, he might have killed me and spared Abul Fazl.

"My Sheikh in his zeal was coming to us
To kiss our feet, but he came without head and feet."

~

Loyalty was not an attribute that could be counted upon at all times. It was a two-way street that had to be continuously nurtured. This was essential to keep the imperial machine well-oiled and in high morale, especially in fierce battles against formidable foes, which took place often. Akbar's conduct assured the men under him that in life and death he stood for them. This impelled them to give their best in the imperial interest.

The departure of the person [Birbal] from this world to the next does not affect us, as the qualities and appearance of the person who has travelled to the other world are etched in our mind. However, even this temporary separation from a person of unparalleled qualities has created a void and caused pain which is beyond words.

—Jalaluddin Muhammad Akbar on Birbal's death

7

Run A Tight Ship... With Mercy and Moderation

Use justice and discretion in this daily market of hypocrisy and double-facedness. Study the action of everyone and be not disturbed by seeing improprieties. Let not love or hate, or threats or encouragements, transgress bounds. A frown will affect with many what in other men require sword and dagger. Difference of religion should not affect assessment of a person's ability and punishment should not be more severe for this reason.

—Akbar to his son Murad while
dispatching him to Malwa

Akbar cultivated a father-son relationship with his subjects. One of his favourite books, *Akhlaq-i-Nasiri*, a 13th-century text on etiquette, ethics and way of life, says: "The ruler is like a gracious, compassionate and sympathetic father to his subjects. The subject should be like the intelligent son and offer his father obedience and respect."

As a loving but demanding father, he administered punishment and granted mercy as he deemed fit. People would tremble in fear when faced with the anger of Jalaluddin Muhammad Akbar because he could be very severe in his punishments. But the punishment was not an end in itself. It was geared towards ensuring compliance and loyalty of the particular wrongdoer and also all potential wrongdoers. The repertoire ranged from minor reprimands to capital punishment to mercy.

Many instances bear out this policy. Once the Emperor asked a *mansabdar* to look for a specific place on the Indus where the river could be forded. The *mansabdar* went upstream twenty-five miles. He asked the people there but could not find the place and thought it pointless to proceed further. He returned and said, "Your Majesty, there is no place where the army could ford the river. A bridge will have to be built."

Akbar asked, "Did you go as far as the place I had told you to?"

When the Emperor learnt that the *mansabdar* had not gone to that spot, he was dragged to that place, bound to an inflated bag of ox-hide and thrown into the river. The entire army saw how he begged the Emperor for his life. When he was carried past the royal pavilion, Akbar pardoned him and had him auctioned as a slave. A friend of the *mansabdar* bought him by depositing money in the royal treasury.

Father Monserrate said of this incident, "This was to set an example for how important it is to obey an imperial command to the last letter. Yet, the crime was not big enough to take the life of a valuable officer...he [Akbar] showed by this example how much store he set by military discipline and obedience. So great an army could indeed have been kept in control by no other method."

Often ways were sought and found to spare the life of the errant. Once the *yasawul*—the officer in charge of arrangements at the court—had fired an arrow at an attendant of the court. When the Emperor learnt of this, a death sentence was pronounced on him. Akbar gave his own sword to Qulij Khan—a very senior *mansabdar*—to execute the sentence. Qulij Khan struck the *yasawul* twice but could not cause any injury. Badshah Salamat accepted that the *yasawul* was destined to live and spared his life. However, as a warning, he was mounted on an ass and paraded.

The Gujarat rebel Masud Hussain Mirza, brother of Mohammad Hussain Mirza, who like Akbar was a descendant of Timur, was brought to the court in a strange state along with about three hundred people. The hides of freshly-slaughtered animals, along with their heads, had been sewn onto the naked bodies of the captives. The prisoners were enveloped in the hides of buffalo, deer, blackbuck, camel, bear, wild goat, cheetah, dog, and horse in such a manner that the heads of the animals were above their heads and the animal skins wrapped around them. As the animal skin would dry and shrink, there was a real possibility of them dying of suffocation. Flies buzzed around them as they begged for their lives. It caused much amusement among the courtiers. But the Emperor ordered that they be freed of the animal hides immediately as he thought a sufficient lesson had been taught.

Even close relatives, howsoever highly placed, were judged on their performance. Raja Man Singh, with whose clan the Emperor enjoyed three generations of closeness and kinship and who was so dear that Akbar called him *farzand*—son—was punished when he failed to live up to the Emperor's expectations. When Maharana Pratap escaped from Haldighati, and there was a perception that he was not pursued with sufficient vigour, as a punishment Raja Man Singh, who had led the royal forces in this crucial battle, was denied access to the royal presence for some time.

How Emperor Akbar treated Mirza Aziz Koka—whose mother had breast-fed the infant Akbar—is a study in temperate behaviour. When this top noble disagreed with the imperial measure of branding—essentially introduced to make *mansabdars* accountable for the mandated upkeep of cavalry forces—he was summoned from Gujarat. When he used intemperate language, Akbar ignored it. Abul Fazl wrote, "As the gracious sovereign had educated him like his obedient children he made as if he did not hear what he said." When good counsel did not help he was confined to his own garden and kept under surveillance. Later the Koka departed for Mecca without imperial permission and sent this message: "There have been powerful Emperors before but nobody has thought of claiming prophethood. Until one has a revealed Book, chosen companions, and miracles, people would never accept it. I can get the title of Azam Khan in the court of the Ottoman sultan for the battles I have fought against the infidels. But I have decided to run a madrasa in His Majesty's name in Mecca. The Emperor may bestow the title of Azam Khan on anybody he wishes."

Badshah Salamat immediately replied to the letter of Mirza Aziz Koka: "When we were expecting Aziz Koka to come to the court to pay respects to us, and earn favours, we learnt that he has left for pilgrimage along with his family and attendants without permission. We are surprised that a sincere companion like him has disregarded the rights of the Emperor. It is also surprising that he had left without his mother's permission since divine worship would yield rewards only with her blessings. What caused Mirza Koka to take such a step?... We are deeply mindful of the services rendered by Aziz Koka's family, especially by his mother Jiji. Instead of anger, we feel pain at Aziz Koka's folly. However, we would not be affected for long. We would not want him to give up the right path or face annihilation in a foreign land. If only Aziz Koka were aware of one-thousandth part of the affection we have for him, he would not have had needless fears. Do not feel encumbered. To please us and for the sake of your deeply distressed mother you can come back even now. This will save you from grief in this world as also the next one. For long we have wanted to send a distinguished ambassador to the Ottoman Sultan to deepen the bonds of love. After this letter we shall write to the Ottoman Sultan. We hope you would return to the court even before the letter reaches him."

Akbar's response to his Koka contained a spectrum in itself—sweet talk, emotional appeal, veiled threat. When the Koka threatened to repair to the rival court of the Ottoman Emperor, Akbar was quick to respond that an embassy would be sent there soon. Akbar was delivering a threat in as civil a manner as possible to a person with whom he had close ties. Given their close relationship, the rebellion had to be handled delicately and even diplomatically. And sure enough, when the Koka came back after some time he was rehabilitated with honour.

It is worth recalling an incident that shows how the Emperor could bring a wrongdoer very close to death yet not execute him. Mirza Mirak, a confidante of the rebel Ali Quli Khan, was brought to the *darbar*. Many others were killed in his presence and then a trained elephant caught him in his trunk, squeezed him and flung him around but did not kill him. This treatment continued for five days before he was finally pardoned.

For the Emperor the virtues of mercy and moderation were never far from his mind when dealing with an errant. The *Akbarnama* says, "In the institutes of sovereignty, and canons of justice, binding and imprisoning are commended for this reason that a trial should be made of ill-fated and contentious people. For man is a strange talisman, and a riddle hard of interpretation. It is not right to send him to the abode of non-existence for one displeasing act which he may exhibit, for this lofty foundation cannot be rebuilt except by the hand of God's power. Therefore, wise administrators have not approved of haste in demolishing and annihilating this high palace.

"For the head of the slain cannot be joined on again."

It also says, "Neither is it the part of enlightened persons to stain a prison with the existence if a man whose evil nature, sedition and strife-mongering, have been several times tested."

The perspective that the Emperor kept in mind when dealing with errants is very clearly articulated by him for the benefit of all—"Sovereignty consists in distinguishing degrees of circumstance and in meting out reward and punishment in proportion thereto. This quality of appreciation adds dignity to the pursuit of happiness and is the chief source of success...In the reciprocity of rule and obedience, the sanctions of hope and fear are necessary to the wellbeing of the temporal government... nevertheless a masterful will, never suffering the loss of self-control under the dominance of passion, should weigh well and wisely the measure and occasion of each."

~

Brutal reprisal to light touch—the imperial HR policies had ample scope and flexibility to fit the need of the hour and to fit the profile of the person to be disciplined. Very clearly punishment was meant to deliver a message to potential and actual wrongdoers but the Emperor never lost sight of the fact that mercy too was an effective tool.

> *The anger of a monarch like his bounty is the source of national prosperity.*
>
> —Jalaluddin Muhammad Akbar
> in the *Ain-i-Akbari*

8

Life After Rebellion?

Only the acute and the truth-discerning know the difference between the good and the evil in the world. Just as poison and medicine both are used in cure, in spiritual remedies as well both kinds of people are needed. Evil ones are encouraged so that they meet their end. What happens if he falls from the wall? What happens if he falls from a hill? If he falls from the highest heaven, he would be reduced to dust. That is, what would happen if he falls from the sky of fidelity to the dusty abode of disloyalty?

—His Majesty's chronicler,
Sheikh Abul Fazl in the *Akbarnama*

Rebellion was a nuanced enterprise in Akbar's India. To seek a better place under the imperial sun or to take sides in succession battles was a challenge to the imperial authority. Looking at prominent episodes, one gets the feeling that obedience and rebellion were not too far apart. A person could rebel, then become submissive and then rebel again. Until one side or both realized that a point of no-return had been reached, the doors of conciliation were not closed.

Akbar's scheme of governance offered a wide spectrum on how to deal with rebels and opponents. They could be met half-way, offered face-savers, their interests accommodated within the larger imperial scheme; or they could be chastised, demoted or exterminated. When it came to sovereignty and the right to rule, a line was clearly drawn. It was non-negotiable. Akbar's grandfather had quoted the Persian poet Sheikh Sadi in his *Tuzuk-i-Baburi*—

Ten dervishes can sleep under one blanket,
But two kings cannot find room in one clime.

Akbar's father Humayun, even when on the run, had refused to give space on the royal carpet to his recalcitrant and ambitious brother Mirza Kamran. Sher Shah had forced Humayun to flee from Hindustan. He had crossed the Ravi river when Mirza Kamran submitted, "Can I sit on a corner of Badshah Salamat's carpet in the presence of Sher Khan's envoy so that there may be some distinction between me and my brothers?"

Humayun wrote back—

Although one's image be shown in the mirror,
It remains always apart from one's self.
It is wonderful to see one's self in another form.
This marvel will be the work of God.

In some cases like that of his half-brother Mirza Hakim he even took care to calibrate his response to ensure that the rebellious brother was not forced to seek external help. It was also part of His Majesty's strategy that rivals and rebels were not delivered into the hands of the foes of the empire. Finally, Mirza Hakim was vanquished but not unseated.

The case of Uzbek nobles within the empire—Ali Quli Khan-i-Zaman and his brother Bahadur Khan were among the prominent ones—offers an interesting case study. They held fiefs in the east and were sometimes defiant and sometimes compliant. The Emperor too played along and would at times use power against them and at times forgive them. Diplomacy was given a chance, often in dramatic ways. Munim Khan Khan-i-Khanan—the top noble who was stationed at Buxar to tackle the rebels—

and Ali Quli Khan-i-Zaman agreed to meet midstream in the Ganga. Both the armies keeping watch on the banks at Buxar, Ali Quli Khan-i-Zaman and Munim Khan Khan-i-Khanan reached the middle of the river in their separate boats. When just a short distance away, Ali Quli Khan-i-Zaman jumped into Munim Khan's boat. Meeting for the first time after the death of Humayun Badshah, they embraced and wept profusely. Both then placed their hands on the Quran and took an oath of loyalty to Emperor Akbar.

However, these diplomatic initiatives did not resolve the issues. Finally, events and circumstances brought His Majesty to a point where he thought that the time for a soft approach was over. The Emperor had, for the time being, tackled Mirza Hakim and driven him out of Lahore; the Uzbek rebels in the eastern part of the empire had declared Mirza Hakim as their Emperor and *khutba* was read, and coins minted, in his name. With this direct assault on his sovereignty, Akbar decided to defy the monsoon and march from Lahore to Allahabad where the two forces met. The rebels were defeated and Ali Quli Khan-i-Zaman was killed on the battlefield. In the words of Mullah Abdul Qadir Badayuni, "With its feet and trunk the elephant ground his bones to powder and made his body like a sack full of chess pieces."

The heads of the two brothers were sent to Agra, Delhi, Lahore and beyond to Kabul as well so that the doubts of all classes of people were put to rest and they saw the fate meted out to those issuing coins in the name of Mirza Hakim.

Akbar's foster brother Mirza Aziz Koka's differences with Akbar over administrative and religious issues would have been met very severely but for the fact that the noble and his mother were very dear to him. Given this delicate relationship, the Emperor treated him leniently. When Mirza Aziz Koka left Hindustan without permission the Emperor wrote to him expressing his concern and displeasure; and when the *koka* returned after some time he was suitably rehabilitated.

But another *koka* (foster brother), Adham Khan, was not so fortunate because his behaviour crossed the limit. His acts of insubordination were met with mild punishment but when he had the Emperor's *atka* (foster father) killed, the Emperor had him flung to death. This was despite the fact that Adham Khan's mother Maham Anga was a very influential figure at the time, whom the Emperor revered.

~

In the Mughal empire under Akbar there definitely existed the option of life after rebellion, though if the rebel miscalculated, and strayed beyond a point, there could be death as well.

As the most choice form of devotion in the social state is to cause the obedience of the proud and stiff-necked by suitable admonitions and vigorous plans, and if advice—"nasihat"—and rebuke are not successful, to remove such from existence so that there may be no crevice in unity, and that the pleasant abode of the world may not be stained by confusion of plurality.

—the Emperor's chief spokesperson
Abul Fazl in the *Akbarnama*

9

Kingship Knows No Kinship

May His Majesty live a hundred and twenty years! Ever since you ordered Adham Khan's killing for the death of your Atka, and of Muazzam for the killing of Bibi Fatima's daughter, people praise you a lot. Your justice was perfect.

—top noble Munim Khan Khan-i-Khanan in the
Tarikh-i-Humayun of Bayazid Bayat,
an employee of Emperor Humayun

It is perhaps the only Mughal miniature where the Emperor's bare torso is visible under a translucent cloth. It shows that he had to emerge from his inner quarters in a hurry to deal with an unprecedented situation. Blood had been shed between two clans closely linked to him. Adham Khan Koka, the headstrong son of Maham Anga—the lady who had nursed Akbar in infancy—had the husband of Jiji Anga, who had breastfed the infant Akbar, killed. The murder happened in the *Diwan Khana* where Shamsuddin Muhammad Atka Khan, the husband of Jiji Anga and Vakil of the empire, was at work. It was a difficult moment for the Emperor. So difficult that he abused Adham Khan in Hindustani and dealt him such a powerful blow that Khan fell. The Emperor then asked his men, "What are you doing, standing idle! Tie this madman's hands and feet."

Despite Maham Anga's powerful role in Akbar's life, and the strong family ties that bound them, ready justice was meted out.

The Emperor ordered that Adham Khan be flung from the terrace. He did not die the first time. So he was thrown, head first, a second time. This time his neck snapped and he died. This incident put an end to the life and career of a *koka* or foster brother, as well as that of his powerful mother Maham Anga. She died of grief shortly afterwards.

In a similar incident, the Emperor heard a complaint that Khwaja Muazzam, who was the step-brother of his mother, intended to kill his wife. The Emperor quickly crossed the Yamuna and reached Khwaja Muazzam's house. When Khwaja Muazzam heard of Akbar's arrival he said, "I will not meet His Majesty."

Just then his wife Bibi Zehra came out of the bath and Khwaja Muazzam plunged his dagger into her. Then, throwing away the weapon, he announced from his window, "Go and tell everyone. I have killed her."

When the Emperor entered the house, he found Khwaja Muazzam's hand on his sword. Jalaluddin Muhammad Akbar said, "What is this? If you try drawing your sword, you will get such a blow on your head that you will not survive."

Khwaja Muazzam lost his strength and sank to the floor. The Emperor then asked him, "Why did you spill the blood of an innocent women?"

When Khwaja Muazzam began babbling nonsense in reply, he was dealt blows and dragged to the river. When the attempt to drown him failed, he was imprisoned at Gwalior Fort where he lost his mind and soon died.

Sometime after this, Akbar asked the prominent courtier Munim Khan Khan-i-Khanan, "What do people say of our sultanate?"

Munim Khan replied, "May His Majesty live a hundred and twenty years! Ever since you ordered Adham Khan's killing for the death of your Atka, and of Muazzam for the killing of Bibi Fatima's daughter, people praise you a lot. Your justice was perfect."

To this, His Majesty replied, "We have done far bigger things. I wonder why people do not mention them. You know of it but do not speak, for it might hurt some people."

Munim Khan said, "How can it be that I keep silent before Hazrat about something I know!"

Jalaluddin Muhammed Akbar said, "I called Atka's clan from Lahore and scattered them like stars and gave them fiefs in various parts of Hindustan. This is far more significant than what you mentioned."

In the course of a trip to Kashmir through difficult terrain, Prince Salim did not escort the royal ladies to join the royal camp because he did not deem the passage safe. Since this was contrary to the Emperor's orders, the prince was denied the honour of paying his respects. An order of censure was served upon Abdur Rahim Khan-i-Khanan, who had been directed to accompany the prince and assist in bringing the ladies—"If the prince, owing to his evil propensities, behaved in this way, why did you allow him to exhibit such audacity?" Royal commands once given had to be complied with at all cost and dereliction of duty could not go unpunished, even though the nature of the punishment could vary.

In the context of a matter that was brought against Akbar's milk-brother Mirza Aziz Koka, Abul Fazl mentions that, "His Majesty...makes no difference between a chief of chiefs and a tangled-haired beggar..."

~

Instances such as those described in this chapter were meant to be signals that the Emperor was a dispassionate dispenser of justice. This image had to be cultivated—and lived up to—for it was part of the charisma that made his rule justifiable.

If I were guilty of an unjust act, I would rise in judgement against myself. What shall I say, then, of my sons, my kindred and others?

—Jalaluddin Muhammad Akbar in the *Ain-i-Akbari,* originally the last part of the *Akbarnama*

10

Be Wary of Close Ones

When one is an Emperor and ruler, one cannot be a brother. If you want to give special treatment to your brother, you must abdicate; if you want to rule, you must forget about being a brother... This is no brother; he is the Emperor's enemy.

—nobles asking Emperor Humayun to execute his rebellious brother Kamran, as quoted in Gulbadan Begum's *Humayunnama,* a text commissioned by Akbar to help Abul Fazl write the *Akbarnama*

It is a popular fallacy that Emperors could take it easy. The fact is that they were always on guard, especially with those close to them. This was especially true of Akbar, who ascended the throne when his father's and even grandfather's contemporaries were still around. And there were strong cliques and factions that resented the authority of the boy Emperor. Bairam Khan, the regent to the young Emperor, himself was a figure that towered over him and reduced the Emperor to a figurehead. Akbar's angst comes out very clearly in the letter of dismissal he wrote to Bairam Khan in the early years of his reign: "Be it known to the Khan-i-Khanan that whereas he has been nourished and cherished by this sublime family and his duties of good service to this court have been ascertained, and as Jannat Ashiyani Humayun Badshah—may God be bountiful to him on account of the good qualities and sincerity which appeared in him—bestowed favours on him, and confided to him the great office of being our guardian, and whereas, after that king had departed from the defiles of this world to the wide spaces of the eternal world, he with loyalty and sincerity bound upon his waist the girdle of devotion and discharged the office of Vakil, we, observing his alacrity in that service, and his seemingly good disposition, left to him the bridle of loosening and knotting to the utmost extent conceivable. Accordingly, whatever he wished, good or bad, was carried out, and thus in these five years some improper acts of his came to light which disgusted everyone... Shah Quli behaved in an offensive manner and did not pay heed to orders, and Muhammad Tahir gave such a rude answer that he deserved to have his tongue cut out or rather to be put to death. He heard of this and did nothing. Lang Sarban uttered before a number of people and in his presence such rude expressions that he too was deserving of punishment...in many assemblages such deeds were performed by him as to distress and trouble our capacious soul. As we wished to please him, and regarded him as a sincere well-wisher of our family, and fully relied upon his words and actions, we considered all these unseemly actions of his as his extreme loyalty and goodwill, and knowingly and intentionally passed them over with consummate benevolence... But as we were ourselves giving our attention to affairs of government, it was considered that he should take his own position and submit what he judged proper, and that then we should according to our judgment pass orders thereon. As we had on various occasions represented that the time had come when we should address ourselves to the duties of sovereignty, it was thought that on hearing of this good news he would be pleased, and that he would be firm and constant in obedience. But it came to our knowledge that he had utterly forgotten the favour which had been shown to him while holding his office, and the claims of our glorious family from their favour and patronage of him during forty years, and from their support of him from his cradle and had hearkened to the words of the rebellious. They [who misled him] for their own selfish objects wished to enlist him among the rebels, and in this last stage of his life to exclude him from other-world joys and to involve him in eternal disgrace. Accordingly, from perfect devilry, baseness and arrogance, they won him over and have carried him off the road. Into the imperial dominions he has introduced dissensions and has endeavoured to extinguish by a cold breath the lamp of the dominion of this family which has been kindled by the eternal radiance, and kept alight by the hand of the divine power. Seemingly the veil of pride and arrogance has blinded the eyes of his understanding, and that he does not know that—

> *"Who blows out a God-lighted lamp,*
> *Sets fire to his own beard."*

Thereafter, the cutting to size of Maham Anga's clan, Atka Khan's clan, the Turanis (who were Central Asian immigrants), the Uzbeks who held fort in the east and were, like Akbar, descendants of Amir Timur, and of course Mirza Hakim, the Emperor's half-brother, who ruled from Kabul, was essential to establish Akbar's own authority. It is not impossible to enter into Akbar's mind and see the reasons why he struck alliances with the Rajputs. These alliances gave him a band of warriors who were loyal and were bound by matrimonial ties, but did not pose a threat to the throne.

The extent of the threat he faced from within his clan is clear from the events around the sacking of Bairam Khan. When Akbar decided to leave Agra for Delhi without telling Bairam Khan, he took along his own cousin, the son of Mirza Kamran. Mirza Kamran was a son of Emperor Babur who had not succeeded in winning the throne and was blinded on Humayun's orders. His son, though not in the line of succession any more, was still of the lineage of Babur and could have been a threat to Akbar if Bairam Khan had chosen to use him.

It is said that Shah Tahmasp of Persia asked Humayun about the reason for his defeat. Humayun replied that it was because of the faithlessness of his brothers. The Shah then pointed at his brother Bahram Mirza, who was holding a bowl and a ewer for the Shah to wash his hands, and said, "This is the way you should have treated your brothers."

~

The act of cutting down to size and weeding out prominent people, clans and cliques was a life-long exercise and was intrinsic to governance. By virtue of their proximity and influence, they could be very troublesome, and because

some had historical ties with Akbar's family, they had to be given a long rope—though the son of Mirza Kamran was soon dispatched to the other world. Fundamentally it was a dispute over power and sovereignty, which for the Emperor was indivisible. Of course, the rebellion of the eldest prince Salim, when he grew up, sorely tested the Emperor's skill in handling such challenges.

> *Shah Tahmasp, the king of Persia…in conversation with Humayun, discussed the question of India, and the loss of sovereignty. He said, "It appears that there are in India two parties who are distinguished for military qualities and leadership, the Afghans and the Rajputs. At present you cannot get the Afghans on your side for there is no mutual confidence. Make them traders instead of servants, and arrange with the Rajputs and cherish them." Akbar recognized that the winning over of this body of men would be one of the great political achievements and strove for it to the uttermost. So much so that he adopted their customs, such as prohibition of cow killing, shaving the beard, wearing pearl earrings, Dussarah and Diwali festivals, etc.*
>
> —Nawab Samsamuddaula Shah Nawaz Khan and Abdul Hayy in *Maathir-ul-Umara*

11

The King Could Do No Wrong

When it was reported to His Majesty that the mines were ready, he had observed that they should be fired from two places lest there should be a delay in the ignition of one of them. Thus he had foreseen the accident with his far-reaching vision.

—His Majesty's most trusted and loyal spokesperson, Abul Fazl, in the *Akbarnama*

Governance is always a complex affair and its pathways are littered with failures, roadblocks and difficulties. How could a person as divinely-assisted as Akbar suffer from such worldly handicaps? Of course, he could count upon Abul Fazl, his official chronicler, to reconcile such contradictions.

A major mishap killed large number of warriors on both sides during the siege of Chittor. Mines were driven up to the foot of the mighty fort and gunpowder was placed on both sides of the Lakhauta Gate. One hundred and twenty *maunds* of gunpowder was placed on one side and eighty *maunds* on the other. The plan was to trigger a simultaneous blast at the two places and breach the wall of the fort. It was planned that the army would enter the fort once it was breached. But there was a single train for both mines and it was fired from one place. Thus, one mine caught fire after the other. This led to an unforeseen accident. The first mine exploded and breached the wall of the fort. The royal soldiers rushed swiftly towards the breach to enter the fort as did the soldiers of Chittor to save the fort. Just then the second mine exploded with such ferocity that it could be heard fifty miles away. Two hundred of Akbar's soldiers and forty of the forces of Chittor were killed instantly. Their limbs were blown away and scattered all over. This was a major setback to the Emperor. Of those who died, twenty were personally known to him.

The siege of Chittor was conducted under the direct supervision of the Emperor. However, Abul Fazl absolved the Emperor of any responsibility for this major mishap. He said, "Before this when it was reported to His Majesty that the mines were ready, he had observed that they should be fired from two places lest there should be a delay in the ignition of one of them. Thus he had foreseen the accident with his far-reaching vision."

Being a chronicler of events, Abul Fazl was duty bound to report what happened. And of course there was a lot happening for which responsibility could be laid at Akbar's doors. But any event that hurt the image of the all-knowing Emperor had to be whitewashed.

For example, when officers whom the Emperor once trusted mounted a rebellion, Abul Fazl wrote, "If His Majesty in accordance with his own secret perception or with the requests of the clear-sighted ones of the court had before this put those evil-doers into confinement, how would the real state of the case have been made manifest to the general public, with whom—the blind and the superficial—rulers have principally to do?"

Reading the *Akbarnama,* one gets a clear impression that the Emperor was the main architect of his rule and every act of his was part of a grand design—"The sage and acute-minded man knows that whenever the lord of the earth forms a right design, and engages in tranquilizing of mankind, the servants of the threshold of fortune become loyal under his auspicious guidance, and with one heart and endeavour recognize the work of their king, their teacher and benefactor, as the Divine command, and devote themselves to his service."

When certain tasks took time to bear fruit, Abul Fazl was constrained to explain—"The few days which wear the appearance of retardation seem to be the result of the Divine wisdom which requires them in order that the inscriptions of the degrees of devotion of the loyal, and the grades of each one's service may be recorded on the portico of visibility, that the jewels of ability may be polished, and the world's lord's method of educating men may be revealed to the world, and that the gold encrusted copper may be placed in the dissolving crucible and the coin of the realm be purified, and that the testing may be carried out to the uttermost."

When Shah Mansur, a key minister who was strict with his accounts, was falsely implicated and hanged, the blame was not laid at the door of the Emperor. Abul Fazl noted the Emperor's regret in the following words—"From that day the market of accounts was flat and the thread of accounting dropped from the hand." And later the loyal chronicler wrote, "there is seldom such an acute accountant and one so laborious, so discriminating...If he had had a little piety to God, a little loyalty to the lord of the universe, some kindness to the people, and a little absence of cupidity and injuriousness, he would never have come to this end from the wrath of the Shahenshah."

In many cases when strong action was the need of the hour but it was delicate to take such action, His Majesty distanced himself from the act. When the rebellious top noble Bahadur Khan, who had been a close comrade of Akbar's father Humayun, was captured in a battle, it was made out that the Emperor wished to spare his life but he was beheaded on the advice of the nobles.

~

In sum, the Emperor had to come out shining in every situation—adverse or favourable—without shifting the spotlight away from him.

> *Those of wide capacity…inflict retribution slowly and with deliberation. Such is the praiseworthy conduct of the sovereign of our age. Under circumspection this class of men [wicked ones] are admitted to the court of fortune. Such gentleness is shown to them that they forget themselves, and open their hands for various kinds of oppression. The Shahenshah in this way makes trial of men and converts poisons—"zehr"—into antidotes.*
>
> —the *Akbarnama*

12

The Contrarian Emperor

It is my duty to have good understanding with all men. If they walk in the way of God's will, interference with them would be in itself reprehensible; and if otherwise, they are under the malady of ignorance and deserve my compassion.

—Jalaluddin Muhammad Akbar in the *Ain-i-Akbari*

Creating space for contrarian and diverse thoughts—including his own—was top of the Emperor's agenda. Under Akbar the state held every one to be equal irrespective of the person's faith and the Emperor was personally inclined to lend his ears to various streams of thought, even if they were contrary to the orthodox opinion at the court. This comes out clearly in the secret chronicle that Mullah Abdul Qadir Badayuni—an ultra-orthodox—wrote: "From childhood to manhood, and from manhood to his declining years, the Emperor had combined in himself various phases from various religions and opposite sectarian beliefs, and had made his own all that can be seen and read in books. Thus a faith of a materialistic character became painted on the mirror of his mind and the storehouse of his imagination, and from the general impression this conviction took form, like an engraving upon a stone, that there are wise men to be found and ready at hand in all religions, and men of asceticism, and recipients of revelation and workers of miracles among all nations, and that the Truth is an inhabitant of every place..."

The Emperor abolished the discriminatory *jizya* tax on Hindus as well as the pilgrimage tax. Marriage to the daughter of the Rajput ruler of Amber, Raja Bharmal, gave Akbar an heir to the Mughal empire—the future Jahangir. The Emperor's ways rattled the ultra-orthodox Mullah Abdul Qadir Badayuni—"Amongst the many wrong and anti-sharia measures he implemented, one was the prohibition to eat beef. The origin of this embargo was that from his tender years the Emperor had often been in company of orthodox Hindus, and thence a reverence for the cow became firmly fixed in his mind, which in their view is the cause of stability of the world. Moreover, there were a whole host of the daughters of eminent Hindu rajas in his harem, and they had influenced his mind against the eating of beef and garlic and onion, and association with people with beards—and such things he then avoided and still does avoid. And he introduced bad practices of Hindus into his assemblies, and still retains them. And in order to gain their love and goodwill and that of their castes, he abstained entirely from everything which was a natural abhorrence to these people. He looked on it as a mark of special devotion to himself if men shaved off their beards—so that this became common practice. And ulema who shaved their beard began to present arguments in favour of it."

The Emperor established an Ibadatkhana—a House of Worship—for multi-faith dialogue about which his chief spokesperson, Abul Fazl wrote, "The wide capacity and tolerance of the Shadow of God were unveiled. Sufi, philosopher, orator, jurist, Sunni, Shia, Brahman, Jati,

Sevra, Charvaka, Nazarene, Jew, Christians, Zoroastrian and others enjoyed exquisite pleasure…The conferences were excellently arranged by the acuteness and keen quest of truth of the lord of the world. Every time, eyes and heart gained fresh lustre, and the lamps of vigil acquired new glory."

The Emperor, as quoted by the Jesuit priest Monserrate, said: "I perceive that there are varying customs and beliefs of varying religious paths. For the teachings of Hindus, the Musalmans, the Parsis, the Jews and the Christians are all different. But the followers of each religion regard the institutions of their own religion as better than those of any other. Not only so, but they strive to covert the rest to their own way of belief. If these refuse to be converted, they not only despise them, but also regard them for this very reason as their enemies. And this causes me to feel many doubts and scruples. Wherefore I desire that on appointed days the books of all the religious laws be brought forward, and that the doctors meet together and hold discussions, so that I may hear them and that each one may determine which is the truest and mightiest religion."

Akbar found unique ways of interacting with people of various viewpoints. He had some of them pulled up on a cot to the balcony near his sleeping apartment. In this manner the brahmin Devi told him about Brahma, Mahadev, Vishnu, Krishna and Ram. Likewise the prominent Sufi, Sheikh Tajuddin was pulled up to the balcony for a conversation. Mullah Abdul Qadir Badayuni wrote, "Sheikh was one of those who weakened His Majesty's belief in our faith."

Even when Akbar wanted people to join Din-i-Ilahi—the order he founded—he did not force his viewpoint. A very close courtier and a relative by marriage, Raja Bhagwant Das and his son Raja Man Singh refused to become followers of Din-i-Ilahi. Raja Man Singh said, rather bluntly, "If discipleship means willingness to sacrifice one's life, I already carry my life in my hands: what need is there of further proof? If, however, the term has another meaning and refers to faith, I certainly am a Hindu. If you order me to do so, I will become a Musalman, but I know not of the existence of any other religion than these two."

The mighty Emperor did not insist thereafter.

However, he did lose his cool and deliver a reprimand when he thought a line has been crossed. This happened when a move was made to invite the prominent nobles Qutbuddin Muhammad Khan and Shahbaz Khan into Din-i-Ilahi. Qutbuddin Muhammad Khan said, "What would the kings of the West say, such as the Sultan of Constantinople, if they heard this? For they all hold the same faith be it a travesty or not."

Jalaluddin Muhammad Akbar replied, "Are you in India on a secret mission from Constantinople that you show such opposition? If you wish to keep a small place warm for yourself, you should go away from India and become an honoured subject there. Leave at once."

On this occasion, an argument broke out between Shahbaz Khan and Raja Birbal, who was a loyal follower of Din-i-Ilahi. An agitated Shahbaz Khan told Raja Birbal, "You cursed infidel, will you go on talking in this manner until I am able to pay you out!"

Badshah Salamat looked angrily at Shahbaz Khan and addressed all those present, "Would that a shoe-full of excrement were thrown into your faces."

His belief in free space for ideas came out very clearly when the Jesuits expressed disappointment at their inability to convert him and wished to go back. At this Akbar said, "How can you say that the time you have spent with us has been profitless, seeing that formerly the Muslims had so much credit in my land that if any had dared to say that Jesus Christ was the true God, he would straightway have been put to death; whereas you are now able to say this, and to preach the same in all security?"

In the body of work Akbar commissioned in stone, text or pictures, or in the words of people who knew him, it is clear that he wanted his people to have a greater sense of—and respect for—diverse traditions. That this was also disorienting for some is evident from the comment of a Jesuit who was at Akbar's *darbar*—"He [Akbar] cared little that in allowing everyone to follow his own religion he was in reality violating all religions."

In the book *Muntakhab-ut-Tawarikh* that he wrote in secret, Mullah Abdul Qadir Badayuni mentions an imperial decree—"No man should be interfered with on account of his religion, and any one was to be allowed to go over to any religion he pleased."

~

It was a remarkable fact of Akbar's Hindustan that you were unlikely to lose your head for holding a belief that others—even the Emperor—did not agree with. Akbar's own views were often at variance with those of the orthodox. This attitude of openness and a respect for contrarian thought had a very healthy effect on governance. It inspired confidence that all could live in peace—*sulh-e-kul*—under the imperial sun and made Hindustan an attractive destination for those forced to leave less tolerant lands.

> *A set of evil-thoughted, shameless ones imagined that the Prince of horizons regarded with disfavour the Muhammadan religion. The sole evidence which those wrong-headed wicked ones, whose understanding was rusted, had for this was that the wise sovereign out of his tolerant disposition and general benevolence…received all classes of mankind with affection. Especially did he search for evidence in religious matters from sages of every religion and ascetics of all faiths. Nor did he accept the replies of the headstrong and unenquiring…*
>
> *When a statement is strong in argument,*
> *It is unfortunate if you do not listen to it.*
>
> —Abul Fazl, about those who raised doubts about Akbar's equitable views towards various sects and faiths

13

Build Bridges with Books and Pictures

His heart is inclined to justice, desiring that the followers of different faiths, each having become acquainted with the truth and reality of others' religion, should act with restraint and abandon bigotry. He has accordingly ordered that the rational contents of different religions and faiths should be translated in the language of each, and that the rose garden of traditional aspects of each religion should, as far as possible, be cleared of the thorns of bigotry.

—Asaf Khan Jafar Beg in *Tarikh-i-Alfi*,
a work of history commissioned by Akbar

Akbar's policy of *sulh-e-kul* (complete harmony) was not merely a talking point. The Emperor took active steps to ensure that the various groups of his diverse empire know each other better. Abul Fazl mentions in the preface of the *Razm Nama*, the Persian translation of the *Mahabharata*, that this was undertaken to enable the learned men amongst Hindus and Muslims to know about each other. He commissioned Persian translations of the *Mahabharata*, the *Ramayana, Yog Vasisht, Harivansa Purana, Sinhasan Battisi* and *Atharva Veda* in order to help build bridges between the faiths.

Akbar took a personal interest in translation and was very sensitive to the need for faithful translation. Faced with a paucity of scholars who were proficient in both Sanskrit and Persian, he found an innovative way around it. He worked at night to understand the meaning of the text of the *Mahabharata* with the help of Devi Mishra, Madhusudan Mishra, Rudra Bhattacharya and Sheikh Bhawan, and then explained it to Naqib Khan, Sultan Haji Thanesari, Mullah Sheri and Mullah Abdul Qadir Badayuni so that they could compile the translation.

Now it transpired that in Mullah Abdul Qadir Badayuni's translation, a saint says before death, "It is right that a man should step out of the limits of ignorance and negligence, and should first of all become acquainted with the peerless Creator, and should pursue the path of knowledge; and not be satisfied with mere knowledge without practice, for that yields no fruit, but should choose the path of virtue, and as far as in him lies, withdraw his hand from evil actions, and should know for a certainty that every action will be inquired into."

His Majesty felt that instead of translating the *Mahabharata* into Persian, Mullah Badayuni had interpolated some issues regarding the Day of Judgment.

"Useless, greedy fellow," the Emperor said in anger.

Mullah Abdul Qadir explained,

"The people of India speak of reward and punishment of good and bad actions. Their beliefs are as follows: when a person dies, the scribe, who writes the chronicle of the deeds of mankind throughout the course of their lives, takes it before the angel, who is the Seizer of Souls, and is called the King of Justice. After he has examined into their good and bad actions, and has seen which has the preponderance, he says, 'This person has his choice.' Then he asks him, 'Shall I first for thy good actions take thee to paradise, that thou mayest there enjoy to the full delights in proportion to thy good actions, and after that send thee to Hell to expiate thy sins; or vice versa?' When that period comes to an end, then he gives orders that the person should return to the Earth, and entering a form suitable to his actions should pass a certain period.

And so on ad infinitum, until the time when he attains absolute release, and is freed from coming into and leaving the world."

The entire court was all ears to what Mullah Abdul Qadir Badayuni was saying. He said, "I am a translator. Nothing more. Whatever the sages of India had represented therein, I had translated without alteration, but that if I had written it myself, I should have been to blame, and should have acted wrongly."

To further disseminate the *Mahabharata,* Akbar asked his nobles to have their own copies made of its Persian translation.

Themes from Christian tradition figured prominently in the paintings made in the royal atelier. At Akbar's behest a book on Jesus Christ called *Mirat al-quds*—The Mirror of Holiness—was written by Father Jerome Xavier in Persian. Father Xavier wrote in the preamble:

"I have related this story because when the Emperor, in whom the world finds refuge, heard of miraculous stories of Lord Jesus, he desired to hear them as they were. As a seeker of truth and lover of knowledge, His Majesty asked this most humble self, Father Jeronimo Xavier, who has had the privilege to present himself at the royal threshold, to commit to Persian all that is there in our books about the sayings and actions of Jesus. Believing that I have done this for forty years and have been learning Persian for seven to eight years, I thought I could render this service. I wholeheartedly devoted myself to this work. Ignoring basic necessities of life and without rest, I got down to fulfilling the command of *zil-i-Ilahi*—the shadow of God—because anything less than this will not suffice to carry out the royal command, especially in matters the hiding of which from people would be unjust and conveying an act of worship. As the Angel Raphael said to Prophet Tobias, 'It is good to keep the secrets of the kings but laudable to clearly tell to all the secrets of God, which would please all.' If I took a long time in writing and copying this book, it really was because, many a time, I would give it a shape and think that the book is complete but when I would match the Persian with Latin books, I would be disheartened and find the work incomplete. With great effort, with the blessings of the Lord and good fortune of His Majesty, the Shadow of God, I finally succeeded and felt satisfied, and had the courage to place it before the true ones. May it be the will of Lord Jesus that His Majesty and others who listen to it feel happy with it.

"I can say that of all works that have been translated into Persian in His Majesty's time, this one is notable. I would not know whether something of this nature has been done before this. Those who knew Persian were ignorant of Latin, or those who knew Latin were ignorant of Persian. And mother earth did not give birth to an Emperor of lofty fortune as His Majesty, who would know and patronize knowledge so much."

~

Akbar was faced with the reality of a society that was diverse and had fault lines. He wanted these diverse traditions not to be at odds with each other. By commissioning translations and paintings the Emperor tried to build bridges across traditions and generate respect for texts of faiths beyond one's own. For a person who was not himself comfortable reading or writing, this was a remarkable trait.

> *There is an inescapable need for synthesis that renders all individuals, cooperating together, comparable to the organs of one individual.*
>
> —*Akhlaq-i-Nasiri*, a book about etiquette and way of life that Akbar liked and recommended

14

Seek Counsel But Be Your Own Man

These loyal ones whose spiritual lamps have derived light from our illuminating flame, may for the present cleanse the slate of their minds from any trace of flattery, and submit proposals of substantial value.

—Jalaluddin Muhammad Akbar in the *Akbarnama*

As we have seen, the Emperor was a great believer in dialogue and deliberation and would go out of his way to ensure that all were at liberty to air their views. Once, to defuse a dispute over the seating plan at a gathering, he proposed that the nobles sat towards the east, the *saiyyids* towards the west, *ulema* towards the south and the sheikhs towards the north and to make all of them feel close to the Emperor he would go to each of them to talk.

In addition to dialogue over matters of faith, he would listen carefully to deliberations on practical issues—his bright eyes keenly observing people—to seek information and knowledge, to know people's minds, and most importantly to create unanimity on issues dear to him.

But both sides knew the rules of the game.

In their utterances, the seasoned courtiers would often factor what they could read of the Emperor's mind. And the Emperor knew how far to go along with the views of the gathering.

Once in the elegant Daulat Khana at Fatehpur Sikri, at his behest the eldest prince and the top courtiers made suggestions for better governance.

Prince Salim said marriages should not happen before the age of twelve.

Mirza Aziz Koka said that governors should not take anybody's life until His Majesty had approved it.

Abdur Rahim Khan-i-Khanan said that lives of small birds and creeping things should not be taken.

Raja Todar Mal said, charities should be distributed at the palace every day and officers should also take care of the destitute.

Mirza Yusuf Khan said, a daily journal of events should be obtained from all cities and towns.

Raja Birbal said, right minded people should be appointed as inspectors in various places to report the state of oppressed people and seekers of justice.

Qasim Khan said, *serais* should be established on the routes throughout the empire for the benefit of travellers.

Sheikh Jamal said, some disinterested and experienced men should be appointed who would bring to court those in distress.

Sheikh Faizi said, experienced people should be appointed to keep a check on the prices of articles being sold.

Hakim Abul Fath said, hospitals should be established.

Sheikh Abul Fazl said, *daroghas* of every city and town should keep a record of householders with their names and trades and keep an eye on their income and expenditure.

Abul Fazl later noted that each of these ten persons had suggested what Akbar had already said on various occasions in the past. If this was so, the nobles clearly took care not to steal the king's thunder even when asked for suggestions.

On one occasion, Akbar sought a stamp on his decisions after he and his *mansabdars* had crossed the Indus in a campaign against his recalcitrant half-brother Mirza Hakim, who ruled from Kabul. After messages of repentance had been received from Mirza Hakim, Sheikh Abul Fazl was asked to ascertain the views of twenty *mansabdars* about the way forward. All of them favoured pardoning Mirza Hakim and returning.

To this Abul Fazl said, "It is proper to finish the work which is nearly completed, and then to punish or forgive."

Although Abul Fazl's opinion angered the *mansabdars* he did not change his view. So it was decided that each *mansabdar* would tell his opinion to His Majesty and unless asked would not disclose the view of Sheikh Abul Fazl. However, after listening to the views of the *mansabdars* the Emperor himself asked about Abul Fazl's views. As luck would have it, Abul Fazl was not present that day and the *mansabdars* said, "He too agrees with our opinion."

An angry Emperor said, "Apparently the officers are afraid of the cold of Afghanistan. I will leave them all behind and go there with my disciples."

The next day the Emperor confronted Abul Fazl and asked, "Why did you change your opinion?"

Abul Fazl said, "Was what they allege me to have said spoken to one person's ear, or was it uttered in the meeting?"

One after another each *mansabdar* said that Abul Fazl had spoken in the meeting. Luckily one *mansabdar* said, "In that meeting Sheikh Abul Fazl was speaking against this set of men."

After this His Majesty set aside the views of the *mansabdars* and moved towards Kabul.

A Jesuit at Akbar's court said, "Before engaging in any important undertaking, he used to consult the members of his council; but he made up his own mind, adopting whatever course seemed to him the best. Sometimes he communicated his intentions to his councillors, to ascertain their views. If they approved, they would answer with the words 'Peace be to our lord, the King.' If anyone expressed an adverse opinion, he would listen patiently, answer his objections, and point out the reasons for his own decision. Sometimes, in view of the objections pointed out to him, he changed the plans he had made."

Sometimes the Emperor would seek the opinion that suited him best. He once asked the *ulema*, "How many freeborn women may one legally marry by *nikah*?"

The *ulema* replied, "It is forbidden to keep more than four freeborn women as wives at a given point of time."

Jalaluddin Muhammad Akbar told the *ulema*, "In our youth we were not particular about this. We married the number of women we pleased, both freeborn or slaves. What remedy can there be for this?"

After hearing various views, Badshah Salamat said, "We have heard from Sheikh Abd-un-Nabi that one of the *mujtahids* had allowed as many as nine wives."

The *ulema* said, "Yes, a *mujtahid*, Ibn-i-Laila was inclined to this. Some had even allowed eighteen from a too literal translation of the verse of the Quran: 'Marry whatever women you like, two and two, and three and three, and four and four.' But this interpretation is rejected."

Badshah Salamat was perplexed. He inquired from Sheikh Abd-un-Nabi, who replied, "I had merely wished to point out that a difference of opinion existed on this. I had not issued a *fatwa* on this."

Badshah Salamat lost his cool and said, "The Sheikh has misled us. He told us at that time a very different thing than what he is telling us now."

To find a way out for Badshah Salamat, the *ulema* gave a *fatwa*, "By *mut'a* a man may marry as many women as he wishes. Such *mut'a* is permitted as legal among those who follow Imam Malik."

There was so much debate on this point that the Emperor called for Mullah Abdul Qadir Badayuni and asked, "What do you think about this?"

Mullah Badayuni replied, "This entire controversy ends at one point. *Mut'a* is legal in the eyes of Imam Malik and the Shiite *ulema*, and illegal in the eyes of Imam Shafi'i and Imam Abu Hanifa. Should a *qazi* of the Maliki sect decide that a *mut'a* is legal, it becomes legal even for the Shafi'is and Hanafis. This is the crux of the matter. The rest is all idle talk."

Emperor Akbar immediately appointed a Maliki as *qazi* who pronounced a *fatwa* for *mut'a*.

~

Akbar encouraged the participation of his courtiers: it was useful to get their input and information on matters of law and governance. But if His Majesty had a strong view, the deliberations had to finally conform to it. In such cases deliberations served the purpose of getting all on board. That his word was final was never in doubt.

> *Although he could neither read nor write, he enjoyed entering into debate with learned scholars. He always entertained at his court a dozen or so of such men, who propounded many questions in his presence. To their discussions, now on one subject, now another, and particularly to the stories which they narrated, he was a willing listener, believing that by this means he could overcome the disadvantage of his illiteracy.*
>
> —a Jesuit account from the court of Akbar

15

Sometimes, Weave a Web

To the extent it is possible to disperse enemies and to root them out by contriving—tadbir—and the use of stratagem, it is not prudent to engage in warfare... There is nothing wrong in creating confusion among one's enemies by resorting to all kinds of stratagems, deceptions and false dispatches but in no circumstances is it permissible to employ treachery—ghadr. The most important condition is to be alert and to make use of spies—jasoos—and scouts.

—*Akhlaq-i-Nasiri*, a book about etiquette and way of life

Life is not straight and simple, and less so for Emperors. The shrewd Emperor knew when he could play straight and when he had to weave a web. There were cliques and forces he could not take on directly. At least not until he felt the time was ripe. Back channels had to be worked and webs had to be woven to deal with them.

When the Emperor sent an invitation to the Portuguese territory of Goa asking for Christian priests there certainly was more on his mind than the stated objective of trying to understand their faith. There were wheels within wheels. It seems he wanted to engage with the Portuguese since they controlled the Indian Ocean trade. The Mughal empire had to depend upon them for Haj travel and trade. Recently tempers had risen when the Portuguese had seized Mughal ships returning from Haj with bullion. Both sides would have seen de-escalation as beneficial. The timing of the Jesuit embassy was especially important for Akbar as he wanted to ensure Portuguese neutrality at a time when he was facing a challenge from his half-brother Mirza Hakim in Kabul.

And there were complexities at home itself, where the presence of the Jesuits was useful to the Emperor. The *ulema* at his court were a powerful presence and there were times when Akbar felt hampered by their views. But the mighty Emperor was conscious of his limits and also that brute force was a last resort. Having provided a forum of debate to the visiting Jesuits and the *ulema,* the Emperor wanted to give the Jesuits the impression that they had his tacit support. So he came up with a backroom solution. Father Monserrate, the Jesuit priest at Akbar's court, wrote:

"[Abul Fazl] is a great companion of the King and a great favourite of his, and in matters of religion he is in the same state as the King. He is the liveliest and keenest mind which I have seen till now. The King said we should speak to him as if with His Highness. We came to understand the great prudence of the King, who in order not to excite his people to rebellion, shows himself to be on their side, and in order that we should not remain without favour, has given orders that this one should always be ours. Thus he carries on being instructed and understanding the things of our faith with as little scandal of his own as possible."

An interesting incident reveals the web the Emperor was capable of weaving, though not always successfully. After a discussion with the Jesuits, the Muslim clerics proposed a fire ordeal. The Jesuits wrote from Akbar's court, "[they] began saying that we should get into fire with the Gospel and they would do likewise with the Koran..."

A fire was made. One of the clerics, whom Akbar

viewed with disfavour, pulled one of the Christian priests by the coat but the priests did not agree to the ordeal. Father Rudolf told Emperor Akbar:

"Since, O King, you desire, with regard to the proposed ordeal to put to the test the constancy of myself and my companions in the faith and religion of Jesus Christ, which we received from our ancestors and drank in with our mother's milk, in which we have been nurtured, and to which we are utterly devoted, we will, with a cheerful heart, and fortified by the help of God, most readily ascend not one but a thousand pyres...Trusting in divine aid, we have no fear of elephants, lions, panthers, leopards, precipices, crosses, stripes, and all manner of tortures. You can prove by immediate experiment, O King, if you so please, whether or not this is true... but if you propose this ordeal of fire in order that you may behold a miracle—as though any one of us were held so dear by God that He would not suffer the fire to do him any harm—we freely confess that, though our trust in God is unbounded, we have frequently fallen into wrongdoing in other respects, and still continue to so fall; for we are sinners, and hence are kept back by grave religious scruples from daring to expect for ourselves miracles, especially when we are ignorant whether God holds us dear or regards us as stumbling- blocks in His way. Moreover, to make trial by fire as to whether or not the Bible is from God, according as to whether or no its bearer are burnt, is at variance with teaching and example of Christ, whom you, O King, honour and esteem... When he was nailed on the Cross and the Jews were asking for a miracle and saying, 'If thou art the son of God, come down from the Cross and we will believe in thee,' even then he paid no attention. As regards ourselves, all those who have suffered torments on behalf of the Faith have been better men than we are. And yet many of them have been burnt. As regards our Book, many Churches and houses containing copies of the Gospels have been burnt by the enemies of our religion; and also many Musalman Mosques containing their sacred volumes have suffered a similar fate. And hence the proof by fire must need be doubtful and uncertain. Now, not to neglect the proposal of the Musalmans, if you definitely order us to undergo the ordeal, we demand that you should release them from their dangerous share in the compact, though indeed, we do not believe that a single one of them would be so faithful to his religion and his Prophet, or so utterly foolish, as to submit himself to such a risk. Indeed their nature is such that they demand miracles; but if a miracle were to be performed by some upright follower of our religion, they would say that it had been brought about by magic and sorcery."

To this the Emperor said, "God forbid that I should have summoned you hither in order that you may suffer any calamity. The Sheikh who wants trial by fire is a criminal and deserves death. We wish him to die in this manner in order not to arouse the people. You please help in this respect and say that you would follow him if he entered the fire first."

When the Emperor proposed his plan in the presence of the Muslim cleric, the Jesuit priests stepped aside with the Emperor and said that they could not cooperate in anybody's death.

Akbar said, "You don't have to undergo the ordeal. I only desire that you say that you would. And if this is not agreeable, you should at least make an affirmative sign with the head."

To this the priests said, "This is not possible."

The Emperor said again, "We will say it in your presence and you could imply acquiescence by remaining silent."

The priests replied, "We cannot do this either."

Akbar said, "We would say it in your absence that you wanted to do this."

The priests said, "You should not do such a thing because, if we were asked, we would have to deny it. If you wish to test our fidelity to our religion you could have us thrown into the fire."

Akbar replied, "We would not do the least harm even to our slaves, much less to you."

The Christian priests said, "If the Sheikh deserves to die because of his crimes, everyone should know it. What need is there of adopting this roundabout course in committing him to the flames?"

Finally, neither the *ulema* entered the fire, nor did

the priests. After that day the Emperor too gave up the idea.

Now what was the Emperor up to? Was the Emperor revelling in the discomfort he had tried to create for the representatives of two organized faiths? Was he weaving a web to see how far the Jesuits could go in taking on the powerful *ulema*? It is possible—and plausible—that something along these complex lines was playing on the Emperor's mind.

~

Clearly there was more to courtly proceedings than was visible on the surface. Complex solutions were being crafted for complex problems—often through the backroom. Weaving a web for adversaries or potential adversaries—within the empire and outside—was very much a part of Akbar's governance strategy.

> *[W]e have learnt that much of what this King did last year and this year was dissembling. He knew that his brother was going to wage war against him. Since he had to personally march against the enemy, he wished to protect his back. This he did by making sure of the Portuguese by a show of attachment to our faith.*
>
> —Jesuit Father Acquaviva in a letter sent from Akbar's court

16

No Power is Absolute

In the cases in which he [Akbar] himself acts as a judge the guilty are, by his own directions, not punished until he has given orders for the third time that this shall be done.

—Father Monserrate, Jesuit priest at Akbar's court

In matters ranging from the routinely administrative to bigger issues of life and death, Akbar tried to ensure that hastiness or impulsiveness on his part or that of his subordinates should not subvert justice or fair governance.

The Jesuit priest at Akbar's court, Father Monserrate, observed: "The crowd of officers, secretaries and paymasters, who administer the royal supplies and grant safe-conducts, passes, contracts, etc., are accommodated in a very large hall. This secretariat is presided over by a chieftain of great authority and ability who signs the royal *firmans*. These are eight days afterwards sealed by one of the queens, in whose keeping is the royal signet-ring and also the great seal of the realm. During this eight days' interval every document is most carefully examined by the confidential counsellor and by the King himself, in order to prevent error and fraud. This is done with especial care in the case of gifts and concessions conferred by the royal favour."

Of course the Emperor himself was deemed above human failings but the royal chronicler Abul Fazl obliquely wrote, "Just rulers and other great ones who have a multiplicity of engagements should not be contented with their own acumen and ability, but should also permit some prudent and well-conditioned man to make representations to them, so that at a time when there is press of work, or when wrath is in the ascendant—which sometimes causes the foot of the wise to slip—he may lay before them suitable considerations."

Towards this end Akbar appointed Abdur Rahim Khan-i-Khanan—a very influential noble who was the son of Bairam Khan and was brought up under royal supervision after the death of his father—to the high office of Mir Arz so that deserving petitions could be presented to the Emperor. It was expected of a person of Abdur Rahim Khan-i-Khanan's stature that he should have the courage to repeat the petitions if he did not receive an appropriate reply from the Emperor.

There were limits to royal power even in matters that caused acute distress to the Emperor. A clear case in point is the way the rebellion of Prince Salim—the future Jahangir—was dealt with. In the last years of Akbar's reign, the prince arranged the assassination of the Emperor's favourite courtier, Abul Fazl. The prince commissioned Bir Singh Bundela to murder Abul Fazl on the suspicion that the latter could be an impediment to his claim to the throne. Abul Fazl was a very close and loyal courtier and his death plunged the Emperor into grief. In a way, the rebellious prince silenced the Emperor's voice since Abul Fazl was the author of the Emperor's ambitious project, the *Akbarnama*, which showcased Akbar's life and deeds. To ease the tension between the Emperor and his eldest son, Akbar's wife Salima Sultan Begum petitioned that she was coming to court with the prince. According to the *Akbarnama,* subsequently completed by another author—"When he [Prince Salim] was approaching the centre of fortune, he sent a petition to the effect that Her Majesty the Queen of the world, Mariyam Makani [the title given by Akbar to his mother Hamida Banu Begum] might take his hand and cast him at the feet of his sphere-brushing Majesty. The petition was granted, and Her Highness Mariyam Makani went forward one stage and by renewed cordiality soothed the prince's terrified soul. Next day he was brought to the palace, and the prince laid the countenance of humility and ashamedness at the feet of the Emperor, wept uncontrollably and confessed his evil doings. The enlightened sovereign ostensibly accepted his inadmissible excuses, and held him in a loving embrace. But this pleading did not remedy the inner dissatisfaction of the sovereign..."

However, when Salim did not mend his ways, Emperor Akbar set out for the prince's base at Allahabad, but had to return to Agra when his mother Hamida Banu Begum fell ill and then died. After this Prince Salim came from Allahabad to offer homage. As the *Akbarnama* says: "His Majesty embraced the rosebush of fortune. The prince presented a diamond worth a *lac* of rupees, 200 *mohurs* each weighing 900 *tolahs,* 200 weighing 50, 4 weighing 25, and 3 weighing 20 *tolahs,* and 200 elephants...As His Majesty was displeased at the ignorance, waywardness, presumption, and self will and other evil acts of the prince, and as although he had many times out of toleration regarded his deeds as if they had not been committed, and what he heard as not heard, yet the prince had from bad companionship and self-indulgence not sought to please His Majesty, he determined at this time to give him a lesson by putting him in prison."

Thereafter the Emperor severely reprimanded the prince and deprived him of wine. Salim's sisters appealed for mercy. After ten days of confinement the prince was released. By now Akbar's only other son Prince Daniyal had ruined his health by excessive drinking, and Prince Murad had already died of the same cause. So the Emperor restored the fief and the ranks of Prince Salim.

In the long saga of princely indiscretions and rebellion, the Emperor allowed himself to be persuaded to revise his decisions, especially since practical considerations dictated that he do so.

~

Behind the carefully created façade of omnipotence was the reality that the Emperor was very much susceptible to pulls, pressures and pitfalls, and had to watch his steps. The exigencies of statecraft and governance demanded compromises, roll backs and sometimes even half-steps.

The administrators of the world have small leisure for forgiveness when they are under the influence of wrath.

Hence it is that far-seeing rulers continually seek out a number of honest servants and give them authority to take the reins of power into their hand at times when wrath is in the ascendant, and enable them to save the guilty by means of making representations... It is an indispensable canon of law that every master should in proportion to his position seek out for himself some servant or other person and have him by him, who may have such a position and trust that he can show courage at such critical moments, and can convey words of truth.

—Sheikh Abul Fazl in the *Akbarnama*

17

See and Be Seen

Whenever he would go with his men to hunt, not only were people accompanying him terrified, even the animals and birds of the area were terrified...Badshah Salamat travelled like this for some months. Although his intention was to hunt, his foremost purpose was to know the state of his subjects. Oppressors were punished. Secondly, he wanted to inspect his army.

—Muhammad Arif Qandhari in the *Tarikh-i-Akbari*, the first chronicle of Akbar's life

Every morning for half a century, except for a few days when he was seriously ill or in grief, Akbar appeared on the *jharokha*—balcony—of his palace or tent, if he were touring, so that his subjects could behold his holy person and start the day with the assurance that all was well with the world.

Akbar's grandfather Zahiruddin Babur wrote that since the age of eleven he did not celebrate two consecutive Eids at the same place. To be constantly on the move was a need of those times.

In a display of both soft and hard power, Akbar wanted to see and be seen across his huge and expanding empire. This enabled him to rule by inspection and *darshan*.

Jalaluddin Muhammad Akbar spent a substantial part of his reign on the move. He travelled in style and on a grand scale with a huge army. The vanguard unit cleared the path, followed by drum beaters and trumpeters on elephants announcing the royal arrival. Behind the Emperor travelled the attendants, the cavalry and then the elephants. When he alighted he was received by a row of elephants on one side and horsemen on the other. It was no less than a moving city that pitched its tents. It was so elaborate that it had to be carried by five hundred camels. The tent put up for His Majesty's use was a two-storied one—called *do-ashiyana manzil*—standing on eighteen pillars. A forty foot high *akashdiya* burnt bright at night, informing people all around of the royal presence. This show of regal panoply and power was intended to impress people into obedience and loyalty.

The Emperor and his entourage—comprising his commanders and soldiers—often hunted, sometimes on a huge scale. As they put a big area under siege and then squeezed the circle to gather the animals in a smaller area, the hunt also doubled up as a war game. It kept the Emperor's army battle ready and also delivered a strong message to the seditious.

His travel plans, his route, and his activities during his tours had strategic significance. When Akbar's rebellious half-brother Mirza Hakim, who ruled Kabul, passed away in 1585, it was feared that one of his sons might be put on the throne or that the Uzbeks might intervene. In this scenario, the Emperor thought it advisable to move towards Punjab, so that his presence sent a message to his adversaries.

The Emperor also took feedback on administrative and revenue matters during these trips. Once he came across a tank and various kinds of trees around it near Sirhind. The Emperor said to the headman, "It seems from your statement that the land was granted to one of the divines who have passed away...What is the present position—how much land is under cultivation and to whom is it assigned?"

The headman replied, "It has one thousand *bighas* out of which seven hundred are under cultivation and has been granted to his son."

The Emperor asked, "According to you his father was a mullah. What is he? Who has given him this grant?"

The headman replied, "People say that he is as learned as his father. This grant has been made by the *sadr*."

After speaking to two more persons the Emperor came to the conclusion that the son deserved the land grant given to him.

It seems Akbar would sometimes appear in the midst of the public in a very informal manner. A Persian traveller named Rafiuddin Shirazi was present in Agra when the Persian ambassador was given a reception in the royal gardens where people had gathered. He wrote: "All of a sudden there was a clamour of 'Badshah Salamat'...I looked to my left and my right but could not find anyone with the appearance of a king. As I turned around I saw, standing there, a young man of about twenty years. He supported his head on one of his hands, which rested on the shoulder of a companion. I guessed he was the king. But the men continued to stand around rubbing shoulders with each other...I asked, 'Is the custom of showing respect not observed at this court? No one has paid respects to the king.' They replied, 'As compared to other realms the tradition of showing respect and observing etiquette is much more elaborate here. But the king is an exceedingly informal person. He often comes out of his private apartment in ordinary dress and mixes with the people around him, making no distinction between friends and strangers. In this situation, how is it possible to observe etiquette all the time?'"

And there were times when he secretly travelled out to ascertain the state of affairs, when he just wanted to see without being seen. Once a large group from Agra had camped outside the city on the way to a shrine. At night the Emperor went to this gathering incognito but was recognized by some petty criminals. To convince people otherwise, he rolled his eyes. Seeing this, people said, "Such eyes and expressions can't be those of an Emperor."

How important it was to be seen in good health was evident when he fell ill. In 1596, he was watching a deer fight when a deer suddenly ran and butted him with its antlers. This lacerated one of his testicles and he was ill for one month and twenty two days. Though Akbar continued to hold public audiences, his illness did cause a commotion.

Likewise, when the Emperor lay dying in Agra, the instability felt in Jaunpur is recorded by the poet Banarsidas in his book *Ardhkathanak*:

> *There was tumult in the city, there was chaos all around.*
> *All doors were closed, traders did not sit in the bazaar.*

Good clothes and good ornaments, all were hidden under the earth.
Account books buried elsewhere, cash and other material safely hidden.
In every home weapons were gathered, people wore ordinary clothes.
Wrapped in rough blankets, women began to dress plainly.
None could make out the difference between the high and the low, rich and poor seemed the same.

~

There was a message in his presence (and also in his absence). The Emperor, being the biggest brand of the empire, had to be showcased and displayed far and wide. To the extent possible, Akbar ruled by the strength of his personality—knowing how to see and be seen, and occasionally to see without being seen.

> *The abode of the empire is cleansed from the weeds and rubbish of disturbance by travelling and hunting, and direct knowledge is thereby obtained of the condition of things. Evil-doers sink into the abyss of failure, and good men acquire distinction. In the second place, districts of opponents become swept and garnished as well as the home-farm of sovereignty, and are enlightened by the glory of justice…the realm grows, diversity changes into unity and the glory of zil-i-Ilahi—shadow of God envelopes mankind.*
>
> —Sheikh Abul Fazl in the *Akbarnama*

18

Gestures and Symbols

Kings and leaders are like a torrent coming down from the mountain top. Whoever tries to suddenly divert its course will not survive. But if a person accommodates himself to it, and in a gentle and subtle manner raises its bank with earth and waste-matter, he will be able to lead it in any direction he wants.

—Nasiruddin Tusi's *Akhlaq-i-Nasiri*,
a text on etiquette and ways of life that Akbar
liked and recommended

In Akbar's *darbar*, communication, both verbal and non-verbal, was nuanced and coded. The communicator and the intended recipient understood what was unsaid, yet significant. The people who worked or followed the king were subtle in their behaviour, and so was the Emperor towards all who interacted with him or who were fortunate enough to see him. Surely people whose lives and livelihood depended upon the Emperor would have closely watched his expressions—his glances, smiles, frowns—and utterances, as well as those of people who were close to him.

Such was the significance of the Emperor's utterances and activities that an entire office, Qanoon-i-Waqia Navis (Office of News Reporting) was set up to record everything the Emperor did or said every day. Those nobles who were not fortunate enough to be physically present in the *darbar* had their *vakil*—representative—to record and send them reports—*akhbarat*—so that they could make sense of the activities of the court.

The elaborate court protocol, including the places assigned to nobles in the *darbar*, was an open display of the supremacy of the Emperor and the hierarchy within the nobility. When the nobles appeared—as mandated—

barefoot and performed *taslim* and *kornish*, it was an act of submission to the Emperor, visible to all who mattered.

When the topmost noble Bairam Khan rebelled and then later submitted to Akbar, what followed was a display of the new power equation: that Akbar had emerged out of the shadows of Bairam Khan, the latter's rebellion had ended and while he was no longer an adversary, his rehabilitation was not on the cards. In accordance with Badshah Salamat's orders, the nobles went out to welcome Bairam Khan. When Bairam Khan kissed the Emperor's feet, the latter took him by his shoulders and raised him. Then Akbar hugged his Khan Baba—as he used to affectionately address Bairam Khan. As a mark of affection, Akbar presented his own robe to him and made him sit at his old place on the right. He was then permitted to depart to Mecca. It is worth noting that it was an honour to be given a place on the Emperor's right side. This entire protocol, enacted in full view of the court, firmly established the primacy of the young Emperor.

The noble Munim Khan, who played a key role in the surrender of Bairam Khan said, "I undertook to assure the Khan that he would be given leave to go to Mecca and Medina."

To this the Emperor replied, "We would have wanted to keep him in our service but since Bairam Khan has made a request we have granted it."

Clearly in this conversation nobody was saying what was actually on their mind. The fact is that Bairam Khan did not have a future in Akbar's service any more. But the conversation was meant to give the impression of a graceful exit.

Such was the sanctity of the Emperor's person that even the imperial *firman* was a symbol of the royal presence throughout the empire. It was accorded respect as if the Emperor himself were present. Abul Fazl's brother Sheikh Faizi, a loyal courtier, wrote to the Emperor:

"After travelling a long distance, I arrived…at a place fifty *kos* from Burhanpur, and the next day pitched my camp and arranged my tent in a manner befitting a servant of the court. The tent was so arranged as to have two chambers; in the second or innermost of which, the royal throne was placed, with the gold-embroidered cushion on it; over which the canopy of velvet, worked with gold, was erected. The royal sword and the dresses of honour were placed on the throne, as well as Your Majesty's letter, whilst men were standing around with folded hands. The horses, that were to be given away, were standing in their proper places. Raja Ali Khan, accompanied by his followers, and the *vakil* and magistrate of Dakhin, approached with that respect and reverence that betokened their obedience and goodwill to Your Majesty. They dismounted some distance from the tent, and were admitted to the outer chamber. They approached respectfully, and were permitted to proceed onwards. When they entered the second chamber, and saw the royal throne at some distance from them, they saluted it and advanced with bare feet. When they arrived at a certain distance, they were directed to stand and make three salutations, which they did most respectfully, and continued standing in place. I then took the royal letter in both hands, and calling him a little nearer, said, 'His Majesty, the vicegerent of God, has sent your highness two royal orders, with the greatest condescension and kindness—this is one.' On this, he took the letter and put it on his head respectfully and saluted it three times. I then said, 'His Majesty has bestowed on your highness a dress of honour.' Upon this he bowed, kissed it, and bowed again. In the same manner he did homage for the sword, and bowed every time Your Majesty's name was mentioned."

When the Emperor wrote to his peers he often dropped hints about the strength of the empire because it was bad manners to openly threaten a fellow Emperor. When writing to the Persian Emperor Shah Abbas, Akbar offered an interesting explanation for delay in correspondence—"The beholding of the honoured letter exuding goodwill sent along with Yadgar Sultan Shamlu in the midst of spring and at the time of equability of night and day made our loving soul to exult. What you have written about the delay in writing letters of affection is very appropriate. In truth, spiritual relationships require that there should not be such delays. But you must have learnt from comers and goers about important affairs and continued wars against the princes of India, which has been reckoned by geometricians as four-sixths of the seven climes. During this long period, this vast country with numerous chiefs and rulers has by divine aid been conquered. From the mountains of the Hindukush to the shores of the ocean all the arrogant rajas, short-sighted Afghan tribesmen, desert-dwelling Baluchi tribesmen, forest-dwellers and zamindars have come under the shade of obedience, and the tribes of mankind have enjoyed equability in concord.

"When Punjab had become the seat of sovereignty it was our intention to send an able ambassador but some urgent expeditions delayed this. The chief of these was the deliverance of the inhabitants of Kashmir from the hands of villainous tyrants. In spite of the strength of the country, and the long marches, the dense forests, the numerous ravines—which can with difficulty be crossed by the forces of imagination—were, by divine aid and blessings of the Imams, traversed by the sublime army in an excellent manner. Several thousand stone-cutters went on, stage by stage, in advance to make the roads, enabling the conquest in a short time. When that splendid country—which is lauded by all who approve of beauty—was granted to us by divine favour, we ourselves went there and offered thanksgiving. We travelled to the hill country of Tibet and then proceeded by the difficult route of Pakli and Damtaur to Kabul and Ghazni. We punished the Afghan plunderers of Swat, Bajaur, Tirah and Bangash, who are a threat to travellers to Turan, and punished the wicked Baluchis and other desert dwellers who are an obstacle in the path of travellers to Persia.

"However, the root of the delay was the confusion in Persia and the distracted state of the country after the death of His Majesty the Shah. When the ambassador arrived with an auspicious message, it became known that the confusion is diminishing."

In this correspondence the subtle message would not be lost upon the Shah that the letter is from a supremely confident military power. In effect, Akbar wanted Shah Abbas to accept the Mughal takeover of Qandhar, a territory that was a bone of contention between the two powers.

When Mirza Suleiman, ruler of Badakhshan since Babur's time, took refuge in India, Akbar rode out at Fatehpur Sikri to receive him. When Mirza Suleiman saw the Emperor he dismounted and ran towards him for *taslim*. Akbar quickly dismounted, prevented him from any formality and embraced him. This ceremony clearly indicated the power equation which was loaded in favour of the rich and powerful Emperor of Hindustan and that relaxing the rule for a senior visitor was a matter of imperial discretion.

The Jesuit priest Monserrate was witness to the arrival of an embassy from the Emperor's half-brother Mirza Hakim from Kabul. This embassy was sent when Mirza Hakim realized that Akbar's son Murad had crossed the Indus along with a powerful force. Emperor Akbar himself was camping on the banks of the Indus but had not crossed it. Monserrate writes—"While he [Akbar] was listening to the embassy, gladiators were fighting with sword and shield, and bison were being pitted against each other. All this had been arranged beforehand in order to create the impression that the King was not engaged in warfare, but was amusing himself as he was wont to do in the circus—the object being to show the envoys how little respect he paid to his brother's power, and how great was the superiority of his court and army."

~

Through verbal, textual (letters, *firman*) and visual (protocol and etiquette) signals and symbols, the Emperor displayed his pre-eminence to the world and subtly conveyed a lot more than was overtly stated. Those whose careers and lives depended upon these signals knew what sense to draw from them and how to respond through appropriate signals and symbols.

> *When His Majesty seats himself on the throne, all present perform kornish and then remain standing at places allocated according to their status, with their arms crossed, partaking, in the light of his imperial countenance, of the elixir of life... The eldest prince stands from one to four yards from the throne, or when sitting, at a distance from two to eight. The second prince stands at a distance of one and one-half*

to six yards from the throne, and in sitting from three to twelve. So also the third; but sometimes the third prince is admitted closer than the second prince… Beyond this, at a distance of three to fifteen yards, if standing and five to twenty if sitting, stand nobles of highest rank who are worthy of His Majesty's spiritual guidance. After this follow the senior nobles at a distance of three and a half yards, and then other nobles at a distance of ten or twelve and a half yards from the throne.

—Sheikh Abul Fazl in the *Ain-i-Akbari*

19

He Was Everywhere!

The spoken word steps forward on man's tongue, and enters, with the assistance of the conveying air, into the windows of the ears of others. It then drops the burden of its concrete component, and returns, as a single ray, to its old place, the realm of thought but occasionally an idea takes a different turn by means of man's fingers, and having passed along the continent of the pen and crossed the ocean of the ink, alights on the pleasant expanse of the page, and returns through the eye of the reader to its wonted habitation.

—Sheikh Abul Fazl in the *Ain-i-Akbari*

Information had to flow both ways in the empire—about the Emperor to the people and about the people to the Emperor. The Emperor had to be the most talked about person amongst his subjects as well as the most informed amongst them.

Even though Akbar was called *zil-i-Ilahi*—shadow of God—he was human and despite wide travel could not be everywhere in physical form. But try he did—through his poets, authors, chroniclers, scribes, musicians, architects and followers. To be everywhere and touch everybody's life, he closely directed the medium as well as the message.

The Emperor was believed to be where his *firman* and gifts were. So special and valued were the Emperor's orders or gifts that they were received with courtly etiquette and courtesies, howsoever far the recipient was from the imperial presence. In that sense they transcended space.

The Emperor's routine sayings and doings were deemed significant enough for meticulous record keeping by *waqia navis*—reporters. Abul Fazl wrote in the *Ain-i-Akbari*: "Their duty is to write down the orders and doings of His Majesty and whatever the heads of the departments report; what His Majesty eats and drinks;

when he sleeps and when he rises; the etiquette in the State hall; the time His Majesty spends in the harem; when he goes to the general and private assemblies; the nature of hunting parties; the slaying of animals; when he marches and when he halts; the acts of His Majesty as the spiritual guide of the nation; vows made to him; his remarks; what books he has read out to him; what alms he bestows; what presents he makes..."

This detailed log was regularly vetted by the Emperor himself and then kept as a record. The Emperor was thus ensuring an authorized version of his daily life. Abul Fazl, in writing his magnum opus the *Akbarnama*—the authorized biography of Akbar and his forefathers—made use of these reports. At His Majesty's advice, eye witness accounts were written by persons who had been familiar with Akbar's father and grandfather. This was to help Abul Fazl write his history. In addition, Abul Fazl also spoke to people who had witnessed Akbar's life. However, in totality, it was Akbar's version. In guiding Abul Fazl to write the *Akbarnama,* Akbar was putting the imperial seal upon the imperial story. It was part of Akbar's attempt to portray his own arrival as a high point of human evolution.

No Mughal Emperor had a bigger *tasvirkhana*—atelier—than Akbar. It was a prolific *tasvirkhana* that painted Akbar's pet themes, giving visual representation to his vision. Obviously this carried his image and vision far beyond his physical presence.

The compositions of musicians and poets he patronized—many of them mentioning the Emperor by name—carried his name far in vernacular. Tansen wrote—

Takhat baitho mahabali, ishvar hoye avtar.
Des des ke seva karat baksat kanchan thar.
Joi aavat soi phal pavat, man iccha pooran adhar.
Tansen kahe saah Jalaldin Akbar,
Guni janan ke kaaj karan koun kiyo kartar.

(The mighty Emperor sits on the throne as incarnation of God.
He serves the land, gifts platefuls of gold.
Whoever comes, gets his wishes fulfilled,
Tansen says of Shah Jalaluddin Akbar,
He has taken birth to do good to the virtuous people.)

Such poetry was meant not just for the Emperor. It was meant to go places—in space and time. Handpicked poets like Faizi gave expression to the Emperor's deepest desires—

"Although kings are the shadow of God on earth, he [Akbar] is the emanation of God's light. How then can we call him a shadow?"

Abul Fazl says that the Emperor himself wrote poetry in Hindi—"The inspired nature of His Majesty is strongly drawn to the composing of Hindi and Persian poetry...He has also strong glorious thoughts in the Hindi language, which may be regarded as masterpieces in this kind." Likewise, his wide interactions with various denominations ensured a lasting place in Jain, Vaishnavite and Parsee literature.

The magnificent Govind Dev Mandir that Akbar's trusted *mansabdar* Raja Man Singh built at Vrindavan had an inscription that carried the message of the Emperor's catholicity—

> *Honourable Akbar in a natural manner nourished the entire earth*
> *So that all were happily following their faiths*
> *Deeming Lord Govind's feet a fit place to reside*
> *The exalted Vaishnavites bless him eternally.*

The musical ensemble called "*naubat*" that played from Akbar's palace or the imperial camp carried the message of the Emperor's presence and wellbeing. The *naubat* was an ensemble of 18 pairs of *damama,* 20 pairs of *naqqara,* 4 *duhul* (all drums of various kinds), 4 *karna,* 9 *surna,* 2 *seeng,* some *nafeer* (all wind instruments), and 3 pairs of cymbals. This sounded five times a day from the *naqqarkhana* placed atop the high gate wherever the Emperor happened to be—in his palace or his camp. Even when the Emperor was on the move, musicians with drums, trumpets and cymbals travelled with him on elephant, camel or boat. This must have lent grandeur to the already formidable entourage.

Forts and buildings that dotted the empire were a constant reminder of the presence of an all-powerful builder-Emperor. The stones were meant to speak of imperial grandeur, invincibility and vision. For example, the city of Sikri that he built from scratch was the king's message in stone. It stood for the synthesis of various traditions—Indian and non-Indian. The Agra Fort that he rebuilt upon an older, and smaller, Lodhi fort spoke of the stability and strength of the empire. Observing the Buland Darwaza at Sikri, one cannot help feeling dwarfed and overwhelmed by its elevation, proportions and majesty. So one can well imagine the impact it had on people when Akbar was alive.

Akbar ruled long—half a century—and ensured that he touched his people's lives in as many ways as possible. The influence of the Emperor was so overpowering that the poet Banarsidas, author of *Ardhkathanak,* fell from the staircase and became unconscious when he heard of the Emperor's demise—

> *In the month of Kartik, Samvat 1662, at the end of the rainy season,*
> *The great Emperor Akbar passed away at Agra.*
> *At Jaunpur, people felt orphaned when they heard this news.*
> *Scared and distressed, their faces became pale.*
> *Banarsi had been sitting on the stairs when he suddenly learnt of Akbar's death.*
> *Shocked, he lost control of himself and fainted and fell.*

He injured his head and bled, the word "God" on his lips.
His head hit the stone floor of the courtyard, which turned red.

While Akbar reached his people in multiple ways, for a reverse flow of information Akbar had his men in the midst of the people. Akbar's favourite book *Akhlaq-i-Nasiri* says, "Informers and spies must continually be employed in seeking out concealed matters, particularly the affairs of enemies, with the ruler ascertaining the opinions of his enemies and opponents from their actions."

The Emperor sought and obtained information about his officers, his subjects and his enemies. In addition to the checks and balances that the administrative system was based upon—which ensured that information from more than one source flowed in—the system had a parallel chain of espionage and reporting. Abul Fazl wrote in the *Ain-i-Akbari*—"He [the governor] should select for purposes of secret intelligence honest, provident, truthful and unavaricious men, and if such needful individuals are not to be obtained, in every affair he should associate several who are unknown to each other and inspecting their several reports thus ascertain the truth."

In his *Dasturul Amal*—a circular on the duties of his officers or standing instructions—Akbar said, "They should be vigilant about spies and not rely on the report of any one of them. For each event it is necessary to get report of a limited number of well-informed spies, each of whom would be unaware of others' reports. The spies who seek popularity should be dismissed and accorded casual treatment."

~

Akbar was meant to be present even when he was not. The paintings that he had made, the giant and elegant structures he built, the poetry and music he patronized and the books he commissioned—the most ambitious one being the *Akbarnama* itself which elevated him to the stature of a superman—were intended to carry his name and deeds far beyond his physical location, and beyond his own physical life. To future-proof his legacy, the Emperor used all means and all available media at his disposal. This large scale enterprise cannot be deemed a failure. Though not in the words and metaphors that Abul Fazl uses in the *Akbarnama,* the Emperor's life and attributes continue to be a subject of discussion and debate till this day. Writers continue to interpret him and try to get into his mind. The present volume is yet another in a long list of books on him. It will surely not be the last.

> *It will not be hidden from the minds of the skilful engineers and artisans that a good name for kings is achieved by means of lofty buildings. It is said, the name of sultans lasts longer on account of their buildings.*
>
> —Arif Qandhari in the *Tarikh-i-Akbari,* the first history of Akbar's reign

20

Best Place to Work

For every employment secure truthful and active-minded men so that they may do good work without desire of money, or of greatness or praise. Do not withhold your own supervision from them. Exalt the right-thinking, and admonish and punish the foolish.

—Emperor Jalaluddin Muhammad Akbar to his son Murad, when dispatching him to Malwa

Akbar's Hindustan—and his court—was seen as a good place to work and therefore attracted the best talent from within and outside the land. The Emperor cast his net wide for capable hands to run and expand the empire. Abul Fazl clearly says, "The first duty of just rulers is to make over countries, where tribes of mankind and various animals abound, to farsighted and just officers of wide capacity, so that the jewel of humanity may be polished and be weighed in the balance of equity, and the administration of justice and the augmentation of dominion may have their proper place." It was believed that Akbar's discerning eye ensured that the best talent was recruited for the best job. Abul Fazl says of him, "From his practical knowledge, and capacity for everything excellent, he can assess men of experience..." The *Akbarnama* gives the example of Khwaja Shah Mansur—who unfortunately became victim of a conspiracy later and was hanged—where the Emperor bypassed the process and relaxed his criteria to promote a person in whom he saw talent.

The Emperor's growing empire offered immense scope for career growth, and he did not discriminate on the basis of faith. While various factors—ethnicity, family connections, strategic considerations, and proximity to the Emperor—mattered in recruitment and rise, Akbar definitely kept his door open to talent from diverse backgrounds, and merit and performance were crucial factors.

The imperial service under Akbar attracted talent from amongst the Rajputs—who were closely bound by matrimonial ties as well—and other groups from Hindu society, in addition to Irani, Turani (which the Mughals themselves were), Indian Muslims and even Afghans (whom the Mughals had unseated). Even Akbar's ministers were drawn from almost all groups within the nobility. By the middle of his reign, Akbar had managed to make his nobility so broad-based that no single ethnic group enjoyed an absolute majority. Even the Turanis, who were the largest group, made up only 24 per cent.

There are many examples which show how persons from diverse backgrounds could climb the imperial hierarchy—sometimes for successive generations.

Raja Man Singh, who was deemed so close that Akbar called him *farzand*—son—was the third generation of Amber royalty serving the empire and was amongst Akbar's topmost generals and administrators. He held important positions like the governorship of Kabul, Bihar and Bengal, and was sent on important military assignments. Raja Man Singh rose to the highest *mansab* a noble could possibly have.

Raja Todar Mal was a Khatri from Lahore and had served in the revenue department of Sher Shah. His expertise in matters of revenue was recognized by the Emperor and he rose to the high office of *Diwan* and also played a crucial role in many military campaigns. Raja Birbal, a close courtier, served the court of Raja Bhagwant Das of Amber and Raja Ramchandra of Rewa before joining Akbar's court and was sent on crucial campaigns. The legendary singer Tansen was poached from the royal court of Rewa. The Emperor spotted an artistic talent in Daswanth, the son of a *palki*-bearer and gave him a prominent place in his atelier.

An irritated Mullah Abdul Qadir Badayuni says, "Hindu infidels, who are indispensable, and of whom half the army, and country, will soon consist of and as to whom there is not among the Mughals or Hindustani Muslims a tribe so powerful, he [Akbar] could not have enough."

Abul Fazl, an Indian Muslim, rose high in the hierarchy and in His Majesty's estimation and was entrusted with the crucial *Akbarnama* project, which aimed at time-proofing the Emperor's legacy.

Mirza Ghiyas Beg, who had fled from Persia, found employment in Akbar's government and rose high. Later, Akbar's son, Emperor Nuruddin Muhammad Jahangir, married his daughter Mehrunnisa and gave her the title Nur Mahal and thereafter, Nurjahan. Mirza Ghiyas Beg attained the high office of Prime Minister under Jahangir. His son Asaf Khan played a key role in the battle of succession after Jahangir's death and sided with Prince

Khurram—the future Shah Jahan. Under Shah Jahan, Asaf Khan rose to the office of Prime Minister like his father.

Muzaffar Khan—a person of Persian origin—was a *Diwan* in Bairam Khan's establishment. When Bairam Khan was deposed, Akbar retained his services despite many nobles advising against it. Muzaffar Khan rapidly rose in the hierarchy and attained the highest office of *Vakil* under Akbar.

Mirza Aziz Koka (Akbar's foster brother) was a Turani and closely linked to the royal family. His father had risen from the position of an ordinary soldier to become a senior noble. Mirza Aziz Koka became the *subadar* of Malwa and Gujarat and held the highest office of *Vakil*.

Munim Khan Khan-i-Khanan, also a Turani, was a close associate of Humayun since the days when the Emperor was driven out by Sher Shah and was struggling to find a place of refuge. He rose to the position of *Vakil* and also the prestigious title of Khan-i-Khanan—the Khan of Khans—and played a key role in the consolidation of Mughal power in the east. The title of Khan-i-Khanan was also held by Bairam Khan, who was the topmost noble in the Mughal hierarchy.

When Malwa was annexed, its Afghan ruler Baz Bahadur—famous also for his knowledge of music—took refuge in various kingdoms for a few years before Emperor Akbar co-opted him into the Mughal imperial service.

The Emperor walked an extra mile to retain the best talent. When the wizard of revenue administration, Raja Todal Mal, wished to retire and spend his last days on the bank of the Ganges, the Emperor sent him a message that no worship of God was equal to the soothing of the oppressed, and that he should spend his last breath in serving man.

Akbar's order regarding Prince Murad's request for transfer of a *dak-chauki* messenger, Bahadur, is worth a special mention. The Emperor said, "Bahadur's wife is not agreeable to going there. If presently we are able to persuade her, we shall send Bahadur as well. Otherwise after a few days we shall depute him to carry a *firman* by *dak-chauki*. Then you may detain him."

While every officer served at the pleasure of the Emperor, Akbar created a systematic organization—a "steel frame", an organized service—in which every officer had a "*mansab*", which in a pair of numbers indicated his rank, salary and military obligations. The *mansabdar* held transferrable jobs and could be given civil or military responsibilities anywhere in the empire. The top nobles also had to remain at the imperial court for some time so that their talent and experience could be appropriately used. This system—and the talent pool it created, nurtured and rejuvenated—ran and expanded the empire and remained effective for at least a century after Akbar's death.

This brings us to a familiar paradox that leaders face. They need bright people to run the place but do not want the limelight to shift away from themselves because that dents their own image. Thus, His Majesty's most loyal and credible voice Abul Fazl is at pains at multiple places to emphasize the primacy of the Emperor's wisdom compared to that of his ministers. He says, "Though the wide capacity and abounding knowledge of His Majesty are beyond needing help, and though the brilliance of the wisdom of this unique one of creation puts the ordinary servants of the Sultanate into the straits of inactivity, yet from his appreciative power, and from his shutting his eyes to the shining of his own God-given beauty, he is ever searching for a good man...and assigns to him the office of a living second soul and a third eye [to Akbar's own]."

When Muzaffar Khan became the *Vakil,* Abul Fazl commented, "Though such an adorner of the throne of realm and religion requires not a Vakil, nor a Vizier, for his far-seeing capacity is responsible for all the duties of sovereignty, yet His Majesty either in order to veil himself, or from humility before God, or in order to increase the dignity of loyal servants, from time to time makes over the duties of sovereignty to a courtier."

Obviously, having the best team in place did not mean that they could be compared to the Emperor himself. As Abul Fazl says, "Good God! The Shahenshah of the age from consummate well-wishing desired to magnify the work of the loyal, and the incomparable Deity willed that all great affairs and noble deeds should be accomplished by that mine of greatness, so that both his grandeur might be certified to all, and also that mercenary servants might have no claim upon him."

Blessing subordinates with power was essential to run and expand the empire but vigilance was advised in the management of the huge apparatus that the Mughal empire had become. There was always the chance of an individual noble or a clique becoming a centre of power. The manner in which Bairam Khan, the topmost noble, had become more powerful than the young Emperor Akbar was never to be forgotten. Abul Fazl writes on behalf of the Emperor—"One of the paramount conditions of authority is that special servants and those in near attendance should abide by fixed rules. In every section of them, there should be prudent persons to oversee their activities, and take precaution against evil companionship, which is the father and mother of wrong ideas, especially when the lord of the age is too occupied with important matters to tend to details. Otherwise, many of the narrow-minded will cease to respect imperial majesty because of their length of service. The wine of familiarity carries them out of their senses. Great seditions emerge from this."

The officers of the state were always under strict watch wherever they might be posted. Father Monserrate wrote, "He [Akbar] did not allow them [officers] to stay in one place for too long; and to prevent them from abusing their power he himself appoints the judges and governors of the cities and towns, who have to report to him how the great nobles behave."

The structure and system devised by Akbar ensured checks and balance. The governors of the provinces were directly under the Emperor. The top team that assisted the governor was also appointed by the Emperor. This team worked with the governor but reported to the respective ministers at the centre. And the central ministers, while having designated portfolios, could only have as much power as the Emperor permitted. The branding—*"dagh"*—regulation ensured that the *mansabdar* maintained the requisite number of soldiers and horses which he was paid for.

The *Maathir-ul-Umara,* an elaborate compendium of biographical sketches of officers of the Mughal empire, notes in the context of the demotion of a noble of Akbar's court—"Wise rulers judge men's nature by their behaviour in games and trifles. Outwardly they keep them in a playful mood, but in reality they are testing him. It is, therefore, essential for courtiers, both while at work and in play, never to ignore the rules of respect and obedience, and a close study of the dispositions of their superiors, who are easily offended, must be regarded as a matter of paramount importance in all their dealings."

To ensure the results he wanted, the Emperor listed clear expectations in writing. He gave a detailed mandate—an SOP—for key positions of administration as has been recorded in the *Ain-i-Akbari.* Despite strict scrutiny and accountability, the Emperor took a balanced view of his officers. Emperor Akbar is once believed to have said, "Todar Mal is very wise and prudent in financial and political affairs, but his unconcern and conceit cannot be approved." But when Abul Fazl, the loyal courtier, made allegations against Raja Todar Mal, the Emperor replied, "I cannot dismiss one whom I have nurtured."

On behalf of His Majesty, Abul Fazl offers the same advice of moderation to the governors—

Court not the world nor to it wholly die;
Walk wisely: neither phoenix be nor fly.

In addition to vigilance and discipline, Akbar also used motivation as a key tool. He could motivate his men and get the best out of them. At a battlefield where his forces were outnumbered, he said, "the enemy appear to be numerous, yet the favour of God towards this supplicant in the Divine Court is greater than man can conceive. It behoves our comrades to hold fast to the cable of Divine favour, and not give place to perplexity or alarm. Let them be of one heart, one face, and one way, and, avoiding distraction, and dispersion, assail the doomed body of troops..."

The battle was won.

By his innovative solutions in various areas—minor to major—the Emperor set a high personal example. In addition to his initiatives noted above and in other chapters, it is worthwhile to recall some more that indicate his attention to detail in various areas:

—Akbar invented a canon that could be carried in pieces and put together again to be used on the battlefield.

—To make the grinding and boring of the barrel of the gun easy, Akbar introduced a device run by animal power.

—According to Abul Fazl, Akbar invented many devices to control elephants. The *loh langar* was a chain that was tied to the elephant's right foot on one end and to a yard-long log, kept near the driver, on the other. This log was dropped when the need arose to control the elephant. In addition, there was a piece of canvas one and a half yards square. The Emperor changed its name from *andhiyari*—darkness—to *ujiyali*—light. It was dropped down over the eyes of the elephant to block its vision. Akbar had three bells attached to this cloth to keep it down. His Majesty began the use of fire crackers to control a rutting elephant. To make the fire cracker called *charkhi,* a hollow bamboo stick was filled with gunpowder at both ends. A stick was put into a hole made in the middle of this bamboo at a right angle, which served as a handle. When fire was put to both ends, it would start turning round, allowing the elephant to be reined back in.

—Under Akbar the *tasvirkhana*—the atelier—fostered super-specialization in line drawing (*tarah*), painting (*amal*), and portrait (*chehra*). It seems this was introduced to get the best artists to collaborate and also to increase the output of paintings.

—It seems that the usage of *khas*-frames to beat the heat was Akbar's invention. The *Ain-i-Akbari* mentions that under Akbar's direction bamboo frames were stuffed with the fragrant root called "*khas*" and water was thrown over it which proved very effective in cooling the air.

—Likewise, Abul Fazl ascribes to Akbar the innovation of using saltpetre to cool water.

~

There was no doubt in anybody's mind that they were recruited by, and served at the pleasure of, one person—the Emperor. Recruitment, posting, promotion, demotion or dismissal were all dependent upon His Majesty, though of course he had his advisors. While being a hard taskmaster, and setting a high benchmark of performance himself, the Emperor could be a discerning, rewarding and motivating employer, which made the Mughal imperial service a sought after employment of that age. Akbar fostered a system which placed a very high value on accountability and performance. This, accompanied by the Emperor's human touch, served the empire and its officers well. It became the best work place in both ways—for the employee as well as for the employer.

There is no throne like Delhi's, no age like Mughal's,
There is no city like Agra.
None as talented as [poet] Gang, none as musical as Tansen,
No ruler like Man [Man Singh] and none generous as Birbal.

No human as [Abdur Rahim] Khan-i-Khanan,
There is no revenue minister as Todar Mal.
In nine continents, seven islands and the seven seas,
There is none like Jalaluddin Shah Akbar.

—Holrai, a poet who was Akbar's contemporary

21

Never Take Office for Granted

Slothful life in retirement does not befit the sovereign.
He grips the world who hastens,
The world is his who delays not,
A king can take rest from everything,
Except kingship.

—Zahiruddin Muhammad Babur,
Akbar's grandfather, in a letter to his son
Nasiruddin Muhammad Humayun

Kingship was a full-time job that did not allow for absence or retirement. It called for full-time devotion. Propaganda about divine rule notwithstanding, Akbar would have known that charisma needs performance to sustain itself, and that he had to be on his toes—literally—for effective rule. For much of his working life he was on the move, crisscrossing his empire, ruling by personal inspection.

Everything he did—or every act of his that was reported—was meant to be in the interest of the empire. For example, he hunted to "acquire knowledge of the affairs of the world, put down oppressors and exalt the good." If there was pleasure in some of these trips, it was always mixed with business.

When he travelled, the office travelled with him and work was transacted wherever he was. In effect, the political capital was wherever the Emperor was—stationary or in transit.

One of his favourite books, *Akhlaq-i-Nasiri* says, "the king's mind should never be free of the thoughts of the management of the realm because his deliberations on how to guard the realm are more effective than the power of mighty armies [*quwat-i-lashkarha-i-azeem*]."

The Emperor had his hands full. As evident from the detailed regulations for issues as diverse as the imperial mint to the food allowed to the elephants, the Emperor kept a close watch over all areas of governance.

The day started early with an appearance at the *jharokha*—balcony—for the benefit of his subjects. So seriously did he take this duty that in half a century of rule the Emperor missed it just a few times—when Raja Birbal died, when he fell from an elephant, when an antelope injured him, when Abul Fazl died, and in the last four days of his life.

Every day he held an open court for a *pahar* and a half—a *pahar* being a span of three hours—where he would dispense justice and listen to the common man. Every afternoon was spent in the female apartments where he heard petitions. In the *Diwan-i-Khas-o-Aam* in the afternoon he inspected the animals, took decisions to grant offices or increase *mansabs*. Special guests and ambassadors presented themselves here. Prisoners of war were also brought here. If the workload demanded it, he remained here till sunset. At nighttime, there were assemblies with learned men. When matters of governance demanded more of his time, each day of the week was assigned to a particular activity. Sundays were fixed for the inspection of horses, Mondays for the inspection of camels, mules and bullocks, Tuesdays for inspecting soldiers, Wednesdays for the business of viziership, Thursdays for dispensing justice, Fridays for receiving people and Saturdays for inspecting the elephant stables.

The Jesuit priest Father Monserrate who had the opportunity to watch him from close wrote: "[H]e amuses himself with various games. These games afford also a public spectacle to the nobility and the common people... They are the following: Polo, elephant-fighting, buffalo-fighting, stag-fighting and cock-fighting, boxing contests, battles of gladiators, and the flying of tumbler-pigeons. He is also very fond of strange birds, and indeed of any novel object. He amuses himself with singing, concerts, dances, conjurer's tricks, and the jokes of his jesters, of whom he makes much. However, although he may seem at such times to be at leisure and to have laid aside public affairs, he does not cease to revolve in his mind the heavy cares of state."

~

Almost everything he did, whether in *darbar* or in public view or in close interactions, was linked to his kingly duties. It would be fair to assume that his mind was seldom free of the affairs of the state, and that he was constantly mindful of the threats and issues that faced him and his realm. This constant preoccupation with affairs of the state was not merely a personality trait; it was an essential job requirement.

> *[Having become the king] he should not increase his hours of comfort and leisure. He should instead*

reduce them and even those he spends in eating, drinking, sleeping and in the company of his wife and children. He should increase the time he spends in work and administration.

—the *Akhlaq-i-Nasiri,* about the duties of a king

22

Ease of Business

Especially see to it that merchants have a good opinion of you for their report carries far.

—Jalaluddin Muhammad Akbar's message to his son Prince Murad when dispatching him to Malwa

Akbar sat at the head of a wealthy empire. And this wealth was in full display at his court. When the ruler of Badakhshan, Mirza Suleiman, came to Fatehpur Sikri to seek help, five thousand elephants, with housings of European velvet and Turkish cloth of gold and chains of gold and silver, were drawn up in a line on both sides of the road. Between each pair of elephants were placed cheetahs with golden collars and coverings of velvet and fine linen, and oxen-cars with fillets of embroidered gold. Also stationed were Arabian and Persian horses with golden saddles. Despite the simplicity the Emperor displayed in his persona, his clothes were worked in gold thread. The *sarpech* on his turban had the ruby from Badakhshan, which his mother Hamida Banu Begum had gifted to him on the occasion of the birth of his first son. Such was his wealth that an estimated twenty crore *tankas* filled in a pond measuring twenty yards in length and breadth and three yards in depth was distributed by the Emperor to nobles, learned and holy men, the poor and the needy over a period of three years.

Knowing that the prosperity of the realm was linked to trade, commerce, and agriculture, the Emperor was at pains to create an environment that would promote ease of business.

Akbar intended to ensure for his subjects, as well as for those of other lands, a protection that is vital for growth of trade and commerce. When he entered Kabul after his half-brother Mirza Hakim had fled from there, according to the Jesuit Father Monserrate who was with him, "Zelaldinus [Jalaluddin Muhammad Akbar] ordered his herald to announce to the people of Chabulum [Kabul] that they need have no fear for their safety: for he fought not with merchants, workmen and common people, but with his brother's army which had now fled."

The Emperor gave detailed instructions for the officers to keep the cities and roads of the empire safe. His Majesty's spokesperson Abul Fazl wrote in the *Ain-i-Akbari*—"[the *kotwal*] shall discover thieves and the goods they have stolen or be responsible for the loss."

Akbar took a keen interest in introducing, expanding and upgrading the production of textile and other crafts, which found their way to the international market from the ports of Gujarat and Bengal (after both the provinces had been annexed by Akbar).

After Gujarat become part of the empire, Akbar also became acquainted with rarities from Europe. A person was dispatched to Goa to get "wonderful goods of that country." A number of skilled craftsmen were also sent along so that new crafts could be imported into the kingdom. When they came back they displayed to the Emperor the arts they had learnt. The *Tarikh-i-Akbari* of Arif Qandhari says, "He [Akbar] has invented new designs of pashmina, silk cloth, brocade, rugs, carpets and he has provided training in the art to expert masters. Consequently these craftsmen now produce such stuff, much superior to those of Iran and Europe."

Under Akbar, the urban centres expanded, as did the nobility which had substantial purchasing power and expensive tastes. The Mughal royalty and nobility became large scale consumers of luxury goods. Mughal cuisine—now known as Mughlai—needed spices which were imported into the empire in large quantities. The empire was a large-scale importer of goods including bullion that was needed to mint coins. Filippo Sassetti, a trader from Florence, wrote, "A prominent ruler of this region, who is a descendant of Timur, who is called the Great Mughal, has a very elaborate court. He is constantly on the move with his nobles. He buys a lot of goods... Whenever any foreigner, whoever and from wherever, alights at Cambay, he is welcomed by four servants of the court, who also make arrangements for their stay and take care of their needs. Then the trader would unload all his goods without any fear. The goods are valued after adding his profit to the cost."

In fact as the Jesuit priest Monserrate points out, "There is a law also that no horse may be sold without the king's knowledge or that of his agents. He allows auctions to be freely held, but buys up all the best horses for himself, without however interfering with the bidding, or taking offence if anyone tries to outbid him. In order to avoid any suspicion of oppression, the money is publicly counted out on these occasions, and the seller receives several gold pieces beyond the actual price."

How Akbar aimed to maximize gains from agriculture and related activities is documented in his *Ain-i-Akbari*. The agrarian data is surprisingly detailed and shows the methodical manner in which the government approached it. Some excerpts from the duties of the *Amal Guzar*—Revenue Collector—in the *Ain-i-Akbari* illustrate the intentions of the Emperor: "[He] should be a friend of the agriculturist...He should assist the needy husbandman with advances of money and recover them gradually...He should ascertain the extent of the soil in cultivation and weigh each portion in the scales of personal observation and be acquainted with its quality. The agricultural value of land varies in different districts and certain soils are adapted to certain crops. He should deal differently, therefore, with each agriculturist and take his case into consideration... He should strive to bring waste lands into cultivation and take heed that what is in cultivation fall not waste. He should stimulate the increase of valuable produce and remit somewhat of the assessment with a view to its augmentation. And if a husbandman cultivate less and urge a plausible excuse, let him not accept it. Should there be no waste land in a village and a husbandman be capable of adding to his cultivation, he should allow him land in some other village.

"He should be just and provident in his measurements.

Let him increase the facilities of the husbandman year by year and under the pledge of his engagements, take nothing beyond the actual area under tillage.

"He should always seek to satisfy the owner of the crops. He should not entrust the appraisement to the headman of the village lest it give rise to remissness and incompetence, and undue authority be conferred on highhanded oppressors, but he should deal with each husbandman, present his demand, and separately and civilly receive his dues.

"He should collect the revenue in an amicable manner and extend not the hand of demand out of season. He should begin the collection of the spring harvest from the Holi, which is a Hindu festival occurring when the sun is about to pass from Aquarius and is entering or has reached mid-way in Pisces and the Autumn harvest from the Dasharah, which is a festival falling when the sun is in the middle or last days of Virgo or the first of Libra. Let him see that the treasurer does not demand any special kind of coin, but take what is of standard weight and proof and receive the equivalent of the deficiency at the value of the current coin and record the difference in the voucher.

"He should stipulate that the husbandman brings his rent himself at definite periods so that the malpractices of low intermediaries may be avoided.

"When there is a full harvest, he should collect the appropriate revenue and accept no adjournment of payments on future crops.

"Whatever is paid into the treasury, he shall himself examine and count and compare it with the day-ledger of the *karkun* [employee]. This he shall verify by signature of the treasurer and placing it in bags under seal, shall deposit it in a strong room and fasten the door thereof with several locks of different construction. He shall keep the key of one himself and leave the others with the treasurer. At the end of the month he shall take from the *bitikchi*—scribe—the account of the daily receipts and expenditure and forward it to the presence. When two lakhs of *dams* are collected, he shall remit them by the hands of trusty agents.

"He shall not make the occasions of journeying, feasting or mourning an opportunity for exactions, and refrain from accepting presents. Whenever a *muqaddam* [village chief] or a *patwari* [village accountant] shall bring money or, advancing to the dais, shall present a *dam* in obeisance, he shall not accept it.

"He shall also waive all perquisites on handicrafts, market-booths, police, travelling passports, garden produce, temporary sheds, enclosure, fishing rights, port-dues, butter, oil of sesame, blanketing, leather, wool, and the like malpractices of the avaricious who fear not God.

"Every month he shall submit a statement of the condition of the people, of the *jagirdars* [persons holding grant of land from which income is obtained], the neighbouring residents, the submission of the rebellious, the market prices, the current rents of tenements, the state of the destitute poor, of artificers and all other contingencies."

~

While the situation on the ground may have been challenging at times—and at variance with the stated intention of the Emperor—documentary evidence does reflect the royal resolve to protect and promote all activities that brought money to the treasury and prosperity to the realm.

> *He should turn his attention to the increase of agriculture and the flourishing condition of the land and earn the gratitude of the people by the faithful discharge of his obligations and account the befriending of the agriculturists as an excellent service to the Almighty. He should retain impartial collectors of revenue and from time to time obtain information regarding their actions. Let him store for himself a goodly reward in the making of reservoirs, wells, watercourses, gardens, serais and other pious foundations, and set about the repairing of what has fallen into ruin.*
>
> —duties of the Sipah Salar—the provincial governor—as given in the *Ain-i-Akbari*

23

Appearances Matter

He shaves his beard, but wears a moustache like that of a Turkish youth who has not yet attained manhood (for on reaching manhood they begin to affect a beard). Contrary to the custom of his race he does not cut his hair; nor does he wear a hat, but a turban, into which he gathers up his hair. He does this, they say, as a concession to Indian usages, and to please his Indian subjects.

—Father Monserrate, Jesuit priest at Akbar's court

Akbar's image was cultivated, recorded and disseminated with a lot of thought. There was a message in how he dressed and looked and what he chose to be doing in the picture. Each portrait portrays a facet of his personality. It never was a picture for the sake of a picture.

The pictures painted in his *tasvirkhana* were monitored by him. His Majesty's voice Abul Fazl wrote, "The work of all painters are weekly laid before His Majesty by the *daroghas* and the clerks; he then confers rewards according to the excellence of workmanship, or increases the monthly salaries."

His was an austere appearance with very little jewellery on his person except earrings and necklaces. But there would be an expensive *sarpech* on his turban, which was a symbol of sovereignty. His *jama*—the flowing upper garment, and the lower garment which he chose to call *yar-pairahan*—friend of the garment—were obviously of the best make. In totality he gave the impression of a man who could afford to dress lavishly but being a man of taste, under-dressed.

Various parts of his persona had meanings that people would identify with. Akbar's turban was different from what his father Humayun and grandfather Babur wore. His headgear was closer to the Rajput headgear than to that of his forefathers. He also chose not to grow a beard, possibly as a mark of affinity to Indian sensibilities. This again was a departure from how his father and grandfather looked.

Around the time he was struggling to assert his dominance over various cliques and factions, he had himself painted holding a cheetah's ears as it was being bound—clearly a man in command of the situation.

Likewise, a miniature displaying tremendous animation—obviously in a still image—is one in which he mounts a fierce elephant and chases another fierce one across an unstable boat bridge on the Yamuna river. This image leaves one marvelling at the Emperor's physical prowess and grit.

The numerous scenes from his *darbar*—in which top nobles are shown kissing his feet or waiting in attendance or ambassadors of foreign powers appearing at his *darbar*—were all designed to bolster the image of an all-powerful Emperor.

When he was shown crossing the Ganga in the rainy season atop an elephant to finally deal with Uzbek rebels Ali Quli Khan and Bahadur Khan, he was delivering a stern message to those who would question his sovereignty. His images in *shikar* or the battlefield—whether leading the campaign against the Gujarat rebels or Uzbek rebels—carried a clear message for seditious elements.

The rebel Masud Hussain Mirza was brought into the Emperor's presence along with about three hundred people, with the hides of freshly-slaughtered animals, along with their heads, sewed onto their naked bodies. There were so many heads of animals in this gathering that when the Emperor had a painting made of this scene, the line drawing was made by Basawan but the colours were filled in by Ustad Mansur, who was an expert in painting animals. The shrinking animal hides would have killed the prisoners but the Emperor ordered that they be freed of the hides immediately. The picture and the story around it speaks of imperial justice that was tempered with mercy.

When he sat listening to a debate between the Jesuits and the *ulema* or when he watched two sects of *sanyasi* fight in a battlefield with the royal soldiers taking one side, he clearly established himself as a person who had a decisive role to play in religious affairs as well.

When he was portrayed travelling on foot to Ajmer to offer prayers at the shrine of Muinuddin Chishti or when he was shown in a trance at Bhera where he suddenly called off a hunt, the Emperor was displaying the spiritual side of his personality.

Akbar was also portrayed as a hands-on Emperor, even visiting and inspecting the construction site of Fatehpur Sikri and interacting with a mason.

Of course it was important to convey the image of a well-rounded personality who was just not a patron of arts but a connoisseur as well. And thus the image of a young Akbar enjoying a dance performance.

~

Akbar himself controlled how he would be portrayed and in what situation because he knew those images would go far—geographically and also beyond his lifetime. So conscious was the Emperor of how he would be projected that he found time, amidst his hectic schedule, to sit for his paintings. For this image-making that he undertook at a giant scale, the Emperor had an atelier larger than that of any Mughal Emperor before or after.

> *Though he was skilled in the art of painting before joining Mughal service, by the Emperor's insight he achieved a high station, and from bringing out mere forms he came to bring out the inner meaning.*
>
> —Abul Fazl in the *Ain-i-Akbari* about Khwaja Abdus Samad, a highly accomplished painter of Akbar's atelier

24

All for *Aql*

He doubts everything and so it is not enough to prove to him the mysteries of the faith with scriptures; he seeks to understand them with reason.

—a Jesuit priest writing from the court of Emperor Jalaluddin Muhammad Akbar

One day Mirza Asad Beg, a courtier, returned from the Deccan with a *huqqa* for the Emperor. This is the first time Akbar had seen a *huqqa*. When he began pulling at it the royal *hakim* tried to dissuade him. The emperor said, "Let me have some to please Asad Beg."

When the Emperor pulled at the *huqqa* two or three times, the royal *hakim* became extremely perturbed and tried to stop him again. The Emperor then handed the *huqqa* to Mirza Aziz Koka. He then asked his druggist about its peculiar qualities who replied, "This finds no mention in our books. But it is a new invention and the stems are imported from Achin, and the European doctors have written much about it."

The *hakim* told the Emperor, "This medicine has not been used before. The hakims have not written about it. What can we tell Badshah Salamat about such unknown things? It is not appropriate for Badshah Salamat to have it."

Mirza Asad Beg told the *hakim*, "The Europeans are not prevented from knowing all about it; there are wise men among them who seldom err. Without having tried it and ascertaining all its qualities how would they prescribe it for rulers and other men—low and high? They must have evaluated its good and bad qualities."

The *hakim* replied, "We do not want to follow the Europeans, and adopt a custom which is not sanctioned by our own wise men, without trial."

Mirza Asad Beg said, "It is a strange thing, for every custom in the world has been new at one time or other; from the days of Adam till now, they have gradually been invented."

Hearing the two sides, the Emperor said, "We should not reject things adopted by people of other nations just because they are not in our books. How would we progress if we do this?" Having said this, the Emperor never smoked again.

Akbar believed that, "The vulgar believe in miracles, but the wise man accepts nothing without adequate proof."

The Emperor was curious about most things—minor or major. He questioned what most people of his age took for granted. It was not sufficient for him to hear that a particular practice had been in vogue from earlier times or had the sanction of religion. He tried to explore the logic behind it. He told his son, Prince Murad, "Every person treading the path of reason is fortunate and one struck in the barren land of tradition is helpless."

Abul Fazl recorded His Majesty's sayings which reflect this bent of mind:

"The faqirs of Hindustan say that keeping death in mind, we should do good work. Not to think of life and one's youth. But we think that good deeds should be done without thought of death. So that we do good just because they are good and not for fear or hope.

"We don't find any reason in the people of Hindustan blowing the conch or ringing the bell in worship. This must be a warning or a reminder.

"Treading the path of reason and rationality is far above the logic this humble self can come up with. If past practices were meant to be followed, the prophets would only have walked in the footsteps of the previous prophets."

To Father Monserrate, the Jesuit priest who had come to the court to convert the Emperor, Akbar asked, "Why is a priest celibate? Is it not a divine command that all men should have wives? You appear either to condemn matrimony or to contradict yourself when you say that celibacy is good and matrimony is also good."

A Jesuit account from Akbar's court puts it very clearly, "Thus we see in this Prince the common fault of the atheist, who refuses to make reason subservient to faith."

Akbar once said, "We do not agree with what people from olden times say that the prophets are put to greatest trial, followed by saints and then good people. Why would God punish his chosen people?"

To this some thinkers said that God does this to test His people.

Akbar replied, "How far is it correct for Him to test when He knows all that is seen and unseen."

Abul Fazl wrote of various causes for misunderstanding among various faiths: "...the blowing of the chill blast of inflexible custom [*taqleed*] and the low flicker of the lamp of wisdom. From immemorial time the exercise of inquiry has been restricted, and questioning and investigation have been regarded as precursors of infidelity. Whatever has been received from father, director, kindred, friend or neighbour, is considered as a deposit under divine sanction."

It seems from what Mullah Abdul Qadir Badayuni wrote in his secret history *Muntakhab-ut-Tawarikh,* Akbar gave this issue serious thought, and

"[A]s a result of all the influences brought to bear on His Majesty, there grew, gradually as the outline on a stone, the conviction in his heart that there are sensible men in all religions, and abstemious thinkers, and men endowed with miraculous powers, among all nations. If some true knowledge was thus everywhere to be found, why should truth be confined to one religion?"

From minor to major matters, he had an original way of thinking. He invented a burning ball to play *chaugan* at night. He conducted an experiment to find out if there is a language that human beings are born with. Babies were secluded from the populace and not exposed to any language to find out if they were born with a *zuban-i-qudrat* or a natural language. Of course, it was a cruel experiment and would not be permitted in a modern society. However it indicates Akbar's desire to arrive at the truth through experiment and observation.

~

In questioning established norms he was definitely trying to create an atmosphere of free enquiry at his court. In the backdrop of his times, his acts and utterances were remarkably rational, even though they unsettled many.

> *Commending obedience to the dictates of reason [aql] and reproving a slavish following of others need the aid of no arguments. If imitation were commendable, the prophets would have followed their predecessors.*
>
> —Emperor Jalaluddin Muhammad Akbar
> in the *Ain-i-Akbari*

25

The Networked Emperor

Impartial statesmen, on seeing the sagacity of His Majesty, blotted out the book of their own wisdom, and commenced a new leaf. But with the magnanimity which distinguishes him, and with his wonted zeal, he continues his search for superior men, and finds a reward in the care with which he selects such as are fit for his society.

—Abul Fazl in the *Ain-i-Akbari*

The Mughal Emperor could be called a networked individual. In fact, networking was one of his prime responsibilities. It was his way of building trust and relationships for the running of an enterprise as difficult as an empire. And this networking started early—much before he became king. Mughal princes had *mansabs* and administrative responsibilities and establishments of their own. In the course of their princely career they gathered experience and built networks which were important to create a base of power. All the resources and experience they gathered and relationships they built was of course useful in the discharge of their administrative responsibilities but came in especially handy at a time when daggers were finally drawn for the battle of succession. In the case of Akbar, two of his three sons—Murad and Daniyal—did not live to fight that battle but they were definitely given responsibilities to prove themselves. Murad had held the position of *Subadar* of Malwa, Gujarat and the Deccan. Daniyal had been the *Subadar* of Allahabad and the Deccan. The surviving son—who was also the eldest—Salim (later Jahangir), was the *Subadar* of Allahabad. He built an effective base and network and started adopting independent airs years before the throne became empty.

For Akbar and his sons, matrimonial relationships were an important part of networking. When, early in his reign, Akbar married the daughter of Raja Bharmal who was the Rajput ruler of Amber—and this was the first in a series of marriages with Rajput royalty—he was laying the foundation of a long partnership. Raja Bharmal, his son Raja Bhagwant Das and grandson Raja Man Singh became pillars of the empire and discharged important administrative and military responsibilities. Raja Man Singh, the nephew of Akbar's wife, was so dear to the Emperor that he was affectionately called *farzand*—son.

When Akbar was on his deathbed, a succession dispute arose between his son Prince Salim and his grandson Prince Khusrau—both men of connections. Salim's mother was the daughter of Raja Bharmal, the Rajput ruler of Amber. Salim himself was married to the daughter of Raja Bhagwant Das, who was the son of Raja Bharmal. Prince Khusrau was born of this marriage. In addition, Salim was married to the daughter of Mota Raja Udai Singh of Jodhpur (Khurram—the future Shahjahan—was born of this wedlock). Khusrau being related to the Amber royalty on his mother's side—the Amber princess married to his father Prince Salim—could count upon the support of his maternal uncle Raja Man Singh. In addition, Khusrau was married to the daughter of Mirza Aziz Koka, a high ranking noble and Emperor Akbar's foster brother, whose other daughter was married to Prince Salim's younger brother, Prince Murad.

And this brings us to another crucial network that bound the Emperor to his foster family. Akbar used to say about Mirza Aziz Koka, "I am bound to him by a stream of milk." Ladies who had breast-fed the infant Akbar were called Anga and were highly respected by the Emperor. Their husbands, called Atka, and their sons, called Koka, enjoyed a high station and had a good chance of rising high in the imperial hierarchy.

It is worthwhile to recall that outside of the royal family only two people enjoyed a *mansab*—rank—higher than all other nobles. These were Raja Man Singh, who was Akbar's nephew by marriage, and Mirza Aziz Koka whose mother had breast-fed Akbar.

There were numerous other ways the Emperor would make or reinforce bonds. When the Emperor bestowed a highly valued honour like the *khilat*—robe—or a title, he was creating a personal bond with that person. The protocol associated with the Emperor created and reinforced his linkages with people. By appearing on the *jharokha*—balcony—every morning of his reign, he created a personal bond with his subjects. The daily *darbar* created a bond with the nobles, the favoured amongst them getting a place to the right of the Emperor. While the princes got to stand nearer, the highest nobles stood at a distance of three to fifteen yards, the next highest from three and a half yards and then the rest of the nobles from ten or twelve and a half yards from the throne. Notably, there was a clear hierarchy in the *darbar*, measured in terms of distance from the place where His Majesty was seated. Those appearing before the king were expected to offer *taslim* or *kornish*. Abul Fazl wrote: "Superficial observers, correctly enough, look upon a king as the origin of the peace and comforts of the subjects. But men of deeper insight are of opinion that even spiritual progress among a people would be impossible unless emanating from the king, in whom the light of God dwells; for near the throne, men wipe off the stain of conceit and build up the arch of true humility... His Majesty has commanded the palm of the right hand to be placed upon the forehead and the head to be bent downwards. This mode of salutation, in the language of the present age, is called *kornish* and signifies that the saluter has placed his head (which is the seat of the senses and the mind) into the hand of humility, giving it to the royal assembly as a present, and has made himself in obedience ready for any service that may be required of him. The salutation, called *taslim*, consists in placing the back of the right hand on the ground, and then raising it gently till the person stands erect, when he puts the palm of his hand upon the crown of his head, which pleasing manner of saluting signifies that he is ready to give himself as offering."

A person was expected to perform three *taslims* upon presenting himself or taking leave, receiving a dress of honour, or a horse or elephant. On other occasions one *taslim* was sufficient. It seems the chosen ones got to kiss his feet and *sajda*—prostration—to the Emperor was practiced in private assemblies.

The court protocol extended beyond the court to any gift or *firman* received from the Emperor. The gift or *firman* was extended deference as if the Emperor himself was present. Howsoever remote the recipients might be from the court, by offering courtesies they bound themselves to the Emperor and became part of his network. This device circumvented the barrier of distance and enabled the Emperor to enrol people in his network wherever they were.

Thus the elaborate court protocol bound a large number of people to the Emperor in a relationship that was unequal—but deemed strong—as the person had offered complete subservience. Akbar sought the highest form of submission from those who chose to join the order woven around the Emperor's personality—sometimes called Din-i-Ilahi. Those who joined took off their turbans and placed their heads at the feet of the Emperor and vowed to sacrifice property, life, honour and religion for the Emperor. Though only a handful of nobles joined this order, it did indicate the direction of His Majesty's efforts—that of creating a very close Emperor-bound inner ring.

The letters the Emperor sent to his nobles were often an exercise in creating or deepening the bond. An example is the letter sent to his prominent noble Abdur Rahim Khan-i-Khanan when the Emperor had received a gift of pigeons from the ruler of Transoxiana, Abdullah Khan Uzbek—"In this way they soar skywards and perform acrobatics, they are incomparable to any species of pigeons known from earliest times till now. Even when a loyal friend like Khan-i-Khanan is absent from assemblies, he should always be remembered at such joyful times. Various groups of pigeons have silently conveyed their greetings to Khan-i-Khanan...They say that their prayers were answered when they got the opportunity to come under the patronage of the Emperor; they were filled with vigour and found a new life. Now they wish to make up for lost years and perform for the Emperor and do not wish to be dispersed. They have thus requested the Khan-i-Khanan—who is devoted to the Emperor—and other well-meaning courtiers to not ask for the pigeons in a veiled manner."

In a letter that was dispatched to Phillip II, the Emperor of Spain and Portugal, but unfortunately did not reach its destination, Emperor Akbar said—"It is not concealed and veiled from the minds of intelligent persons who have received the light of divine aid and are illuminated by the rays of wisdom and knowledge, that in this terrestrial world, which is the mirror of the celestial, there is nothing that excels love, and no propensity so worthy of cultivation as philanthropy, because the peace of the world and harmony of existence are based upon friendship and association; and in each heart illuminated by the rays of the sun of love the world of the soul or the faculties of the mind are by them purged of human darkness; and much more is this the case when they subsist between monarchs, peace among whom implies the peace of the world and of the denizens thereof. Considering these things we are with the whole power of our mind earnestly striving to establish and strengthen the bonds of love, harmony and union among the population, but above all with the exalted tribe of the princes who enjoy the noblest of distinctions in consequence of a greater share of divine favour, and especially with that illustrious representative of dominion, recipient of divine illumination, and propagator of the Christian religion, who needs not to be praised or made known; and this decision is on account of our propinquity, the claims whereof are well-established among mighty potentates and acknowledged to be the chief conditions of amicable relations. But as weighty obstacles and great hindrances have delayed personal intercourse, an exchange of messages and correspondence is the best substitute for it... We entertain hopes that the portals of correspondence will be continually kept open on both sides, whereby we may inform each other of various affairs and pleasant hopes."

In an age when the Mughal emperors never undertook international travel, Akbar's letters to fellow kings of Iran, Transoxiana, Spain and Portugal was an exercise in diplomacy and bonding—in addition to pursuit of strategic goals.

As seen above, Akbar's network, while being large, was hierarchical as well. It gave more access and privileges to some. After all, the privileged feel privileged only when others are denied the exclusivity they enjoy. Abul Fazl wrote in his introduction to the *Ain-i-Akbari*, "...

the wise ones have counselled that visionary princes do not appoint every lowly person to their service; of the ones thus appointed, not everyone is admitted daily into the Presence; amongst those upon whom this privilege has been conferred, not everyone becomes entitled to proximity in conversation; of the ones arrived at this junction in the palace-garden of privilege, not all are to be permitted familiarity of address; among those so honoured, not everyone is admitted into the august assembly; of those upon whom this ray of fortune falls, everyone is not allowed into the assembly of secret counsel; among the carriers of this blessing, not all obtain place in the exclusive council of advisors."

~

Akbar was truly a remarkable leader in trying to create systems. But the system could not be above personalities. It had the Emperor at its heart and institutions were only as good as the people who manned them. Thus, it was important for the Emperor to have his relationships with people—and continuously work on them—to ensure that the needs of the empire were met.

> *We hope that knowing that our loving heart is disposed towards every kind of subject and enterprise, the Shah will tread the beautiful path of correspondence and diurnal reports.*
>
> —Jalaluddin Muhammad Akbar's
> letter to Shah Abbas of Persia

26

Larger Than Life

God has bestowed upon the people such a great boon and blessing in the holy personality of Hazrat Badshah. Because of his nobility and his excellent administration, Hazrat Badshah had become the leader of the spiritual world.

—the loyal cleric Sheikh Mubarak,
when the Emperor returned to Sikri
after a major victory in Gujarat

Taken together, all the attributes mentioned in the preceding chapters made Akbar larger than life.

Being larger than life was not merely a matter of personal vanity. It made rule and governance easier. It gave people confidence in the Emperor's right to rule. For the Emperor, it ensured compliance with very little fuss. Faith in the Emperor's right to rule placed him on a pedestal beyond the reach of mortals. However, the sharp Emperor knew the truth about his clothes. He had to guard against doubters including those who believed that his authority should cease where that of religious men began, and also those amongst the nobility who did not believe in his absolute authority.

So his image-making was a job constantly in progress. The Emperor himself said, "The very sight of kings has been held to be a part of divine worship. They have been styled conventionally the shadow of God, and indeed to behold them is a means of calling to mind the Creator, and suggests the protection of the Almighty."

This image building had to be actively done by others around him, for it would not behove the Emperor himself to harp upon his divine right to rule. The best brains of the land were involved in creating and reinforcing the image of the supreme leader and of course taking on those who were seen as an impediment to this grand imperial project. Prominent amongst the loyalists was a family that was deeply devoted to him and his larger-than-life image. This was the prominent cleric of his time, Sheikh Mubarak, and his two sons, Faizi and Abul Fazl. When the Emperor was tired of the authority of the *ulema,* Sheikh Mubarak told him, "Your Majesty is the *imam* and *mujtahid* of the age. What need have you of these *ulema* for assistance in issuing your commands, whether religious or secular." While reading *khutba,* which he could not complete, the Emperor announced from the pulpit of Jama Masjid in Sikri that he was subordinate to none in matters worldly or spiritual. Sheikh Faizi wrote a poem from which the Emperor was able to recite three couplets—

In the name of God who gave us sovereignty,
Who gave us a wise heart and a strong arm,
Who guided us in equity and justice,
Who expelled every thought from our heart except justice.
His attributes are beyond comprehension,
Exalted be His Majesty, Allahu Akbar.

It seems the Emperor lost his nerve at the pulpit and left his *khutba* unfinished. But the larger task continued. Soon all prominent clerics of the kingdom were forced to sign a document drafted by Sheikh Mubarak that gave the Emperor superior authority over religious affairs.

To project and then preserve for posterity the image of a superman he entrusted to the most loyal courtier Abul Fazl a massive project called the *Akbarnama*. True to his mandate, Abul Fazl saw in his master a divine light. This history of Jalaluddin Muhammad Akbar and his ancestors was aimed at proving that the world was blessed to have a divinely ordained Emperor—a theme that runs through several volumes.

Abul Fazl wrote, "Kingship is a gift of God and is not bestowed till many thousand grand requisites have been gathered together in one individual...It is clear to the wise that a few of the holy qualities are magnanimity, lofty benevolence, wide capacity, abundant endurance, exalted understanding, innate graciousness, natural courage, justice, rectitude, strenuous labour, proper conduct."

In the same vein Abul Fazl's brother, Faizi—also a loyal courtier—said:

This king, whose wisdom shows the path to God,
He is an ocean, inseparable even for a moment from God,
People call him the shadow of God,
I say, not shadow, he is the divine light.

Another close courtier and the most prominent musician of the age, Tansen, wrote:

Takhat baitho mahabali, ishvar hoye avtar.
(The powerful king sits on the throne,
As an avatar of God.)

Abul Fazl projected an aura around the Emperor and even traced his lineage to the mythical figure Alanqoa who was impregnated by a divine light. The descendant Jalaluddin Muhammad Akbar himself was seen as somebody who had miraculous powers and superhuman foresight. The Emperor was seen as worthy of complete submission. This was symbolized in the ceremony of placing one's head at his feet when people were initiated into Din-i-Ilahi, the order that Akbar founded around his own personality.

Alongside this project was the elaborate protocol that governed the Emperor's relationship with all around him and beyond. He appeared at his *jharokha* at dawn everyday—barring a few days of illness or grief, every day in half a century of rule—so that his subjects could start the day with a look at the auspicious face. Court protocol dictated that all courtiers stood barefoot with hands folded while the Emperor sat. There was a *saiban* (parasol) above him to indicate that the subjects were under his protection and also various other insignias of power including arms and standards close by. Elaborate rules were laid down for the distance the courtiers (and even the princes) had to keep from the Emperor, and the manner in which they had to offer obeisance like doing *kornish* or kissing the Emperor's feet, which was a special privilege. The Emperor's *firman,* wherever received, or a *khilat* (robe) when received as a gift had to be accorded the respect that was given to the Emperor himself.

According to a Jesuit account, "[The Emperor] would have people believe that he performs miracles, healing the sick with the water with which he washes his feet. Many young women pay vows to him to get their children cured, or that they may have children. And if these things come to pass, they bring him offerings, as to a saint, which, though they may be of little worth, are willingly received and highly valued by him."

Once Akbar was informed that a traveller had encountered a tiger which had leapt to take his life. The man drew a line around himself and called upon the name of the Emperor. Hearing the name of the Emperor, the tiger stood still and the man escaped unhurt.

He was also called *mahabali*—the powerful one—and this image is captured in the pictures he commissioned. One has him holding a cheetah by its ears as it is being tied. Another has him mounted on an unruly elephant to chase another powerful elephant across the Yamuna river over a shaky bridge of boats.

Abul Fazl mentions instances of people having visions of the Emperor in the midst of the battlefield and their fortunes immediately being restored.

The *Akbarnama* mentions a battle where Akbar himself came under attack while on an elephant—"Seven [arrows] hit the Shahenshah's shield. He used to say that five went through and through his shield to the extent of three and five fingers and that two stopped in the shield without traversing it. The Divine protection was another shield which protected him."

Akbar was also larger than life in his large-hearted view of people. The Emperor said, "an enemy should not be despised…since friendship and enmity are but phantasms of the divine dispensation, one should overlook the intervening enemy and view the deity beyond."

~

As *zil-i-Ilahi*—shadow of God—Jalaluddin Muhammad Akbar knew that it is important to do great things but even more important to be projected as a person who is destined to do great things. The message was clear to all who might harbour seditious thoughts—why waste time taking on a person who has the backing of divine forces or—as Abul Fazl writes—was the *peshwa* (leader) of the spiritual world.

> *The profound and the judicious had perceived, from the dawning of the Shahenshah's personality, that he was the epitome of the volumes of perfection and had recognized him as akin to the spirit of holiness and as a gatherer of wisdom of the Divine school.*
>
> —Sheikh Abul Fazl in the *Akbarnama*

27

After Me, Who?

This chaos lasted ten days, then there was peace.
A letter received from Agra said all was well.
It said, Emperor Jalal ruled for fifty-two years,
Now in the month of Kartik Samvat 1662, he died.

—poet Banarsidas on
Akbar's death in his *Ardhkathanak*

Every person in authority faces a question of, to use the current jargon, "succession planning": who will take his seat when he is not around in mortal form. Without fail, it is a tricky issue for more reasons than one. Akbar groomed Prince Salim for higher responsibilities but this also placed resources at the disposal of the prince to challenge the Emperor.

Secondly, no leader is powerful enough to manage the aftermath of his own death. When the throne falls empty the Emperor is not around to smoothen the path for his chosen candidate. In a way, despite his best efforts, the field is thrown open.

Emperor Akbar's last years must have been disappointing. If he wished his three sons to be tested on merit, such expectations were dashed. All three occupied high offices under the Mughal state and were expected to prove themselves worthy of the highest office. But the two younger brothers of Prince Salim died of alcohol abuse. Even while alive they were often a source of much anguish to the Emperor. And after the two died, Prince Salim, being the only surviving son, was seen as the inevitable choice, though still a source of trouble, including on account of his intemperate consumption of alcohol. The prince had the backing of the Emperor's mother and other relatives whose views could not be easily brushed aside. But complex forces were at play in the Emperor's last days. Prince Khusrau, the eldest son of Prince Salim, emerged as a contender and the tension was visible between father and son.

For Akbar's amusement a fight was arranged between Prince Salim's elephant Giranbar and Prince Khusrau's elephant Aprup. After many rounds, it seemed that Prince Salim's elephant Giranbar had the upper hand. When the royal elephant Ranmathan was brought in to stop the fight, Prince Salim's attendants threw stones and mud at the elephant driver to stop him. Prince Khusrau ran and complained to the Emperor who asked Prince Khurram, presently seated beside him, to go to Prince Salim.

With utmost politeness, Prince Khurram told his father Prince Salim, "Shah Baba is saying that you have won this elephant fight. Then why this attack and inappropriate behaviour?"

At this Prince Salim replied, "We are not aware of this. Neither did we order an attack on the elephant or its driver, nor do we approve of it."

Prince Khurram replied, "If it is so, please allow us to separate the elephants with fire crackers and other means."

Bans—firework rockets—and *charkhi* were fired, after Prince Salim authorized it, but to little effect. Ranmathan and Giranbar jumped into the river, fighting. Giranbar was not ready to give up the fight. But a large boat drifted up suddenly between the two elephants, making Giranbar unable to launch any more attacks.

Prince Khurram went back and clarified to the Emperor, "It was a wrong report. He did not approve or order this."

Akbar, however, was left perturbed by this rivalry between his son and grandson.

While Emperor Akbar was on his deathbed, a serious effort was made to secure the succession for the Emperor's grandson Prince Khusrau by the latter's father-in-law Mirza Aziz Koka and maternal uncle Raja Man Singh. Calling all the nobles together, Raja Man Singh and Mirza Aziz Koka said, "The character of the high and mighty Prince Sultan Salim is well known, and the Emperor's feelings towards him are notorious; for he by no means wishes him to be his successor. We must all agree to put Sultan Khusrau on the throne."

As soon as this was said, a prominent noble of the empire, Sayyid Khan said, "Of what do you speak, that in the existence of a prince like Salim Shah, we should place his son upon the throne! This is contrary to the laws and customs of the Chaghatais, and shall never be."

Finally, with the support of the nobles, the crown passed to Prince Salim, though this was not the end of Khusrau's rebellion.

~

The effort to bypass Salim did not succeed but the very fact that an effort could be made while Akbar was still alive—though dying—shows the limits of royal power as far as the question "Who will come after me?" was concerned. That Khusrau continued to pose a problem to the new king long after his coronation shows that the issue of succession had to be settled by the contestants and not by the dictates of the previous ruler. After all the battle of succession was a test of the various qualities that a candidate needed to run an empire. And in that respect, the best man won.

> *Corrupting ideas had crept into Khusrau's mind in consequence of his youth and the pride youths have, and the lack of experience and lack of foresight of worthless companions, especially at the time of my revered father's illness. Some of these short-sighted ones, through the multitude of their crimes and offences, had become hopeless of pardon and indulgence, and imagined that by making Khusrau a tool they might conduct the affairs of the state through him. They overlooked the truth that acts of sovereignty and world rule are not things to be arranged by the worthless endeavours of defective intellects…*
>
> *He who is seized of Fortune cannot be deprived of it;*
> *Throne and crown are not things of purchase;*
> *It is not right to wrest crown and dominion*
> *From the head which God, the crown-cherisher, has indicated.*
>
> —Emperor Nuruddin Muhammad Jahangir
> in the *Tuzuk-i-Jahangiri*

28

Code of Conduct for Administrators

(A Summary of an Imperial *Firman*)

Sometimes a foolish person can solve the problems of the wise.

—from the *firman*

"This venerable *manshur* [royal communication] and guidance provides *dasturul amal* [an administrative manual, in effect 'standing orders'] emanating from the mine of imperial bounties, addressed to all experienced administrators and managers of the state such as the auspicious sons, devoted members of the royal family, *amirs* of exalted rank, all *mansabdars, amil* and *kotwals*. They are required to abide by the following instructions everywhere in the administration of towns, villages and *katra* [markets].

"They should neither seek seclusion like dervish, neither mix with general people too much...A middle path is recommended. They should be vigilant in morning, evening, midnight and midday.

"In leisure hours they should read books on ethics and morals.

"Best service to God in this world is the growth of relations and the accomplishment of works of people's welfare which should be performed without regard to friendship, enmity or relationships.

"They should be helpful to the best of their ability to the poor and downtrodden, particularly the retired and the recluse. They should seek the company of God-fearing recluses.

"They should carefully examine the faults and crimes of people...They should distinguish which fault is pardonable and which cannot be ignored. Disobedient people or recalcitrant chiefs should be guided to the right path through exhortation, admonition or mildness of generosity. If exhortation or persuasion fails, resort to imprisonment, beatings and amputation of limbs keeping in view the position of the person.

"They should not rush into capital punishment as the verse says, 'a severed head can never be joined.' In such cases the criminal deserving capital punishment should be sent to court...If there is a delay in receiving the king's order or in the criminal's dispatch or that detention may cause tumult, they may deal with the offender at their own level. But they should not flay or trample the criminal under the elephant since these punishments should only be given by great kings.

"Punishment should be given according to the status of the offender. For a noble person a mere stern look could be tantamount to capital punishment, while even beating may not be helpful for a lowly person.

"They should allow privacy with wise and honest people who can draw their attention towards the faults of administration. They should patronize men who have the courage to speak truly, for such men are rare.

"They should not entertain flattery beyond a point except insofar as it is indispensable for it is sometimes unavoidable for servants.

"Give personal hearing to appellants as it is said, 'Do not leave appeal of a person to the *Diwan* for perhaps the petition is against the *Diwan* himself.' Petitioners should be summoned in order of arrival so that the first entrant does not have to wait unduly.

"They should make suitable enquiries before awarding punishments because reports may be incorrect as deceitful people are numerous and the truthful rare.

"They should not swear, for it is likely to invite imputation of motives of falsehood and thereby create doubts in the minds of believers who trust them. Expressing bad words is a mean habit.

"Develop agriculture by encouraging the cultivators and giving them loans so that villages and towns flourish. Collect revenue in such a manner that it encourages people to bring all cultivable land under the plough, which would increase prosperity. After this take steps to maximize superior crops. Make individual enquiries from cultivators about minutest matters.

"Ensure that neither the soldiers nor anyone else tries to enter a person's house without permission.

"Always consult wise men. If such are not available they should still consult: 'Sometimes a foolish person can solve the problems of the wise.'

"What can be assigned to servants should not be assigned to sons. What can be assigned to sons should not be done by self because what is neglected or spoiled by others can be repaired by themselves but if something is destroyed by their own hands, it would be difficult to rectify it.

"Accepting apologies and overlooking faults should be part of their nature. No one is without fault. An admonition often emboldens a person, while at other times it can lead to vagrancy. A person may have to be punished for first fault, while in others a thousand faults may be forgiven. Punishment is one of the most delicate acts of statecraft and should be tackled wisely and cautiously.

"Do not interfere with religious matters, customs or beliefs of people, for as a wise man would not intentionally choose his own loss in transient worldly affairs, how could he deliberately select a wrong path in eternal matters? If men are right, officers should not oppose them. If they are not right, they should not be opposed since they deserve sympathy rather than opposition or oppression.

"Do not bear ill-will against any person… Every act of friends and foes should be considered as emanating from God as the hearts of both are in His custody.

"Do not joke or laugh too much.

"Sleep or food should not exceed limits.

"Be vigilant about spies and not rely on the report of just one of them. For each event it is necessary to get report of a limited number of well-informed spies, each of whom would be unaware of others' reports.

"Wicked and mean people are useful against their own kind but should be kept in check so that they do not harm good people.

"Exercise vigilance over associates and servants lest they oppress people, and over glib and cunning flatterers who in guise of friendship cause disturbance and enmity. While grandees are preoccupied these mischief-mongers have plenty of time for such activities.

"Popularize philosophy and learning.

"Extend patronage to old families.

"Wisest is one whose expenditure is less than earnings.

"Do not become residents in assigned places... Be willing to be summoned to court.

"Do not be too fond of hunting but do go out hunting occasionally for military exercise and relaxation.

"Make effort to keep prices low and do not allow rich men to hoard and raise prices.

"*Kotwal* should be the guardian of law. He should keep record of residents of each household in every *mohalla*. There should be a *Mir-i-Mohalla* in every *mohalla,* who should be consulted on matters related to the *mohalla*. There should be a spy in every mohalla. Persons like *Sahib-i-Mohalla* and *Khabardar* [a government employee who has the duties of a guard] should assist men in distress. Nobody should embark on a journey without informing *Mir-i-Mohalla,* Khabardar and the neighbours. Nobody—stranger or relative—should stay in the *mohalla* without informing the *Mir-i-Mohalla*. A person not having a personal bail should be settled in a separate inn.

"Quietly seek information of income and expenditure of people. If their expenditure exceeds their income there is certainly something wrong, which should be honestly investigated.

"Take bail from each category of brokers and ask them to report all sale and purchase transactions in the market. Names of buyers and sellers should be registered in the *roznamcha* [daily diary].

"Appoint *chauki-i-shab* [night patrol] in every *mohalla* and bylane and near cities.

"Try to eliminate thieves, pickpockets and swindlers from your jurisdiction. If unable to recover plundered or lost goods, you should make good the loss.

"Make every effort at prohibition. However it is permissible if meant for use as a medicine or a stimulant to increase intellect.

"There should be separate passages to the river waters for men and women."

29

Dawn of a New Age!

If in my admiration of you I were to call you the second Sikandar [Alexander], it would be just and fair because you have given better protection to your kingdom and subjects than that even provided by Sikandar.

—Arif Qandhari in the *Tarikh-i-Akbari*,
the first chronicle of Akbar's reign

It seems written all across the massive work, *Akbarnama*—needless to say, articulated by His Majesty's most obedient spokesperson, Abul Fazl—that a new age had dawned with the reign of Akbar; in fact, with the birth of Akbar.

As if to drive home the point, Akbar instituted a new calendar starting from the beginning of his reign, clearly marking it as an epochal event.

The *firman* proclaiming the launch of the new Ilahi era was drafted by Abul Fazl—"God be praised! During this mighty sovereignty there have been in the visible world so many great events and shining actions, such as the subjugation of great cities, and the complete capture of impregnable forts and other victories, and divine aids, any one of which was fit to be made the foundation of an era. But if Your Majesty directs that the new era commence from the day of your seating yourself on the throne of sovereignty, which was one of God's great gifts and never-ending boons, and from which auspicious day this is the twenty-ninth solar, and the thirtieth lunar year, assuredly such a good deed will be at once a mark of thanksgiving and a fulfilment of the wishes of mankind. Moreover, there is not involved in this good deed any breach of the respect due to the glory of the *Hijri* era—which comes from the day when His Majesty, the best of men, migrated from Mecca to Medina on account of the predominance of foes. This is the supposition of worthless persons infirm in nature and of mean understanding."

Abul Fazl goes into raptures describing the succession and coronation of young Akbar that followed the accidental death of his father Nasiruddin Muhammad Humayun—"The Sultan of the spheres [the sun] had reached the auspicious House of Pisces, and had bent his sublime aspect towards his House of Exaltation, in order that he might make the four-pillared throne of Aries radiant with the auspicious Accession, and might refresh the dust-stained denizens of earth's domain by universal plenty. A canopy of trees threw a shade over the parterre which made the throne-chamber; and the King Rose [*Khusrau-i-Gul*] sat on an emerald throne, wearing a diadem composed of the hundred-leaved rose, set with jacinths and rubies; and sweet voiced birds, like the heralds of an imperial accession, with scarves of long feathers [*shahpar*] on their bodies, and ermine robes on their bosoms, raised high the *khutba* of joy from many-pillared arboreal pulpits. The cypress and the pine, who stood in respect's antechamber, bowed their heads in reverence, and the box tree and juniper, who were feeble and needy seniors, put on the dress and the airs of youth. Glorious tulips and aromatic plants donned parti-coloured robes, and the young tulips and dog-roses could not for joy contain themselves in their vestments. The sound of the drums of thunder, set upon the heads of elephant-clouds, made uproar throughout the seven climes, and the pearl-dropping voices of early spring emitted a general invitation to the four quarters of the universe. The winds of enduring bounty began to issue from the blow-holes of benevolence, and the flower gardens of the Divine Caliphate blossomed anew. Meanwhile the moon was bonding the brow of supplication in adoration and thanksgiving, and was gathering light by the hand of Cassiopeia, and the Polestar was anointing the two eyes of the Calves with white antimony from a pencil of golden rays."

The loyal spokesperson Abul Fazl performs a deft act. He extolls the virtues of Akbar's father Emperor Nasiruddin Muhammad Humayun and yet says that the perfect one—Akbar—had arrived on the scene.

Abul Fazl wrote: "Good God! How could it enter into the circle of thoughts and imaginings of the farseeing that a being so wondrous in his perfections and so befriended of fortune, at once the arranger of the visible world and the acquired of spirituality, should so soon leave this earth? But as the time had come when the Creator would give rejuvenescence to the old world and give a new education to mankind—a time which had not arrived in many cycles of the past—of necessity He designed to exhibit the nobly-constituted and consummate paragon who shall be the perfection of mortals. Consequently the occurrence of this unavoidable event, though in the eyes of the superficial a subject of mourning and sorrow, might be reckoned by the eyes of the mature of vision as a treasury of glory and beauty. For by the bounteous presence of this sublime pearl of sovereignty the visible and invisible worlds became again glorious, and the market-square of dominion, spiritual and temporal, became active."

And then he wrote something startling: "If the ruler of the age [Humayun] had on account of his right-seeing and good qualities been preserved in the prison of visible life, it must have followed that, on account of the submission to the noblest, which is proper according to the rules of wisdom, this eminent one of the age [Humayun] should submit to the nursling of light [Akbar]. But as the robe of fatherhood is an imposing one and cometh from God, it could not harmonize with obedience to the offspring. Also the happiness of children cannot be recorded in the book of fate except when they submit to their fathers and obey their behests. Consequently it was unavoidable that the beginning of the feast of fortune should be the lord of earth's leaving this world."

Thus without taking anything away from the meritorious predecessor Emperor Nasiruddin Muhammad Humayun, Abul Fazl projects his untimely death as a necessary evil since he had to make way for an Emperor whose time had come.

Likewise, Nizamuddin Ahmed, the author of a history of Akbar and his predecessors—including the kings of the Delhi Sultanate—was embarrassed about the sequence he followed in his book. He wrote, "although it is fit that a description of the events of the reign of His Majesty

[Akbar] should be the prefatory beginning of all books, not to speak of this one, yet as he [the author] has had a chronological arrangement before his eyes, he makes the narration of the auspicious events of His Majesty's reign, the end of the section about the Sultans of the court of Delhi, which is the centre of Hindustan."

~

Even though many of his predecessors were his own ancestors, it was obviously important for Akbar to sell the idea that his was an age like never before. People who counted themselves blessed to be living in Akbar's age were likely to be dutiful and grateful subjects. And that was the idea!

> *[T]he great Emperor, the Sultan of the Sultans of the world, the beneficent shadow of God, the vicegerent of the Omnipotent, the strengthener of the pillars of world-conquest, the founder of the rules for governing the world, the ruler of the world and of all who inhabit it, the lord of all time and of all that exists in it, the embodiment of Divine secrets, the personification of spiritual essences, the most potent conqueror and the most successful ruler, the lion in the wilderness of political and religious warfare Abul Fateh Jalaluddin Muhammad Akbar Badshah Ghazi...*
>
> —Khwajah Nizamuddin Ahmed in the *Tabaqat-i-Akbari*, a history written in Akbar's time

30

The End

Hindu women fetch water from their rivers, tanks or wells, and many of them bear several pitchers one above the other upon their heads and converse and chat freely with their companions, walking the while over any inequalities of ground. If the heart in like manner preserves the balance of its pitchers, no harm will befall them.

—Jalaluddin Muhammad Akbar in the *Ain-i-Akbari*

If I were keeping vigil as Akbar lay dying, I would have said, "Here goes a man who stood for moderation." If you read closely the statement of a Jesuit who was at Agra at that time—"None knew in what faith he lived or died"—you would know that he was many things to many people because he gave space and time to as many voices as he could. And tried to find meaning in them.

Of course, this puzzled many at his court and beyond.

Earlier in his reign when the Jesuit priests first got an opportunity to observe him, Father Rudolph Acquaviva observed in a letter, "People here have various views about the King. Some believe he is a Christian, others that he is a Hindu, and others a Muslim. Some other people with better judgement think he is neither a Christian, nor a Hindu, nor a Muslim. In my view this is true, or perhaps he is a Muslim, but conforms to all to win the goodwill of all."

Making the point very clearly in a letter to Shah Abbas of Persia, Akbar himself said, "The Creator has decreed that the kings are guardians of all mankind. Men do not intentionally make mistakes. Why would they be negligent in the affairs of faith and religion, which are permanent and everlasting? The position of every sect comes under one of the two categories. Either it is in position of truth, and in that case one should seek directions from it and accept its views. Or it is in the wrong, and then it is unfortunate and suffering from ignorance, and is a subject of pitying kindness, not harshness and reproach. One must exercise wide toleration so that friends are not destroyed under the idea that they are enemies, and enemies masquerading as friends will not have an opportunity for deceit."

Seeing the world from various perspectives and also enabling people to hold their own perspective—isn't this the foundation of great CEO-ship?

~

Out of wisdom he constructed a loom
With knowledge for brocade, and speech for beauty
The warp he made of soul, and the wool of eloquence,
The dye he took from thought, and the broidery from sense.

—Abul Fazl in the *Akbarnama*

A Brief Timeline

1483: Birth of Zahiruddin Muhammad Babur.

1508: Birth of Nasiruddin Muhammad Humayun.

1530: Death of Babur. Coronation of Nasiruddin Muhammad Humayun.

1539: Sher Shah defeats Humayun in the Battle of Chausa.

1540: Sher Shah again defeats Humayun in the Battle of Kannauj.

1541: Humayun's marriage to Hamida Banu Begum.

1542: Birth of Jalaluddin Muhammad Akbar.

1543: Humayun and Hamid Banu Begum leave for Persia. Young Akbar falls into the captivity of his uncles.

1556: Death of Humayun. Coronation of Jalaluddin Muhammad Akbar.

1560: Bairam Khan is relieved of his post.

1561: Bairam Khan is killed. Akbar's victory over Malwa.

1562: Akbar's first visit to Ajmer. Marriage to the daughter of Amber's Raja Bharmal.

1563: Tax on pilgrimage is abolished.

1564: Assassination attempt on Akbar. Uzbek revolt. Death of twin sons Hasan and Hussain. Construction of Agra Fort begins.

1568: Chittor victory.

1569: Ranthambhor victory. Birth of Salim.

1570: Murad is born.

1571: Construction of a new city in Sikri begins.

1572: Gujarat victory. Daniyal is born.

1573: A lightning march of nine days from Sikri to Ahmedabad. Ahmedabad victory.

1574: Sheikh Abul Fazl and Mullah Abdul Qadir Badayuni arrive at the court. Attack on Patna. Victory over parts of Bihar and Bengal. To log all the activities of the Emperor a new office of records is established.

1575: Ibadat Khana built. Weekly debates on religion begin.

1576: Battle of Haldighati. Bengal victory.

1578: A big hunt is organized in Bhera. Akbar's state of trance.

1579: Akbar attempts to read *khutba*. Akbar's last visit to Ajmer.

1580: Mirza Hakim's revolt. First group of Christian missionaries reaches the court.

1581: Mirza Hakim is defeated.

1582: Pope Gregory XIII writes letter to Akbar. Din-i-Ilahi is founded. Persian translation of *Mahabharata* begins.

1584: Beginning of Ilahi calendar.

1585: Akbar leaves Sikri. Kabul is annexed after the death of Mirza Hakim.

1586: Abul Fazl is directed to write *Akbarnama*. Victory over Kashmir. Akbar makes Lahore his capital. Raja Birbal is killed.

1587: Birth of Khusrau. Persian translation of *Ramayana*.

1589: Death of Raja Todar Mal. Death of Raja Bhagwant Das. Miyan Tansen's death. Victory over Sindh. Translation of *Tuzuk-i-Baburi*.

1592: Qandhar victory. Odisha victory. Birth of Khurram—the future Shah Jahan.

1599: Death of Prince Murad.

1600: Ahmednagar is won. Salim revolts.

1601: Akbar returns to Agra.

1602: Sheikh Abul Fazl is assassinated. On Akbar's order, a book is written in Persian on Jesus Christ.

1605: Death of Prince Daniyal. Death of Jalaluddin Muhammad Akbar. Coronation of Nuruddin Muhammad Jahangir.

Glossary and Explanations

Ain-i-Akbari: "Regulations of Akbar".
akashdiya: A lamp that was lit at a tall height in the royal camp.
Akbarnama: "Book of Akbar".
Amir: A noble of high rank. Its plural is *umra*.
Anga: Foster mother who had breastfed the Emperor.
Atka: Foster father; husband of Anga.
Badshah Salamat: It was the phrase by which the Mughal emperor was addressed. It means the same as "God Save the King".
bigha: A measure of land area.
Chaghatai: The Mughals were also called Chaghatai because they traced their lineage to Changez Khan's son Chaghatai.
dam: One-fortieth of a rupee.
darbar: Royal court.
Diwan: The minister in charge of the administration of finance.
fatwa: It is a formal legal opinion given by a mufti in answer to a question.
firman: Written edict of the Emperor.
hakim: Physician.
Ibadat Khana: House of worship or devotion.
Imam: A preacher; one who leads the congregation in prayer.
jama: A robe worn by men with a tie fastened under one shoulder.

jizya: A tax imposed on non-Muslims in an Islamic regime.

Khan-i-Khanan: The highest title a Mughal noble could achieve.

khilat: Robe of honour.

khutba: Friday sermon at the mosque which mentioned the ruler's name.

koka: Foster brother.

kornish: A formal salute to the emperor.

mansabdar: Mughal civil servant.

Maryam Makani: One who is equivalent in station to Mary.

mast: An elephant in heat.

Mirza: A princely title given to all Timuri males.

mufti: A canon lawyer of standing who is authorized to issue a fatwa.

mullah: Person leading Muslim prayers.

mut'a: Temporary marriage.

qamargah: A way of hunting in which a large area is surrounded and beaters progressively shrink the circle until the game is trapped in a small area.

qanoongo: Hereditary keeper of revenue records.

qazi: A person who dispenses justice in accordance with Islamic law.

sheikh: A title of religious dignity; religious divine; complimentary epithet for Indian Muslims.

Subadar: Governor of a province.

Sulh-i-kul: A policy of amity for all.

taslim: Formal kowtow before the Emperor.

Vakil: Highest minister at the imperial court.

waqia-navis: Record keeper.

yasawul: Officer in charge of the arrangements at the court.

Further Reading and Gratitude

There are three vantage points for Akbar-watching between 1556 CE, when he took the throne, and 1605 CE, when he died in office. One is that of Abul Fazl, the loyal historian of Akbar. His is an official account and is rich in factual information. Its merit does not lie in its objectivity, because it is not an objective account. Its viewpoint is very clear and it is valuable for that reason. It tells us how Akbar wanted to be seen by people in his lifetime and after. So the multiple volumes of the *Akbarnama* give us Akbar's perspective on himself.

Quotes and information from the *Akbarnama* are primarily derived from the following translations: Henry Beveridge's translation of *The Akbarnama of Abul Fazl*, 3 volumes (Kolkata, 2010); Heinrich Blochmann's translation of *Ain-i-Akbari*, Volume 1 (Kolkata, 2010); Henry Sullivan Jarrett's translation of *Ain-i-Akbari*, Volumes 2 and 3 (Kolkata, 2010). I have also benefited from the *Akbarnama*'s latest translation by Wheeler M. Thackston (and the accompanying Persian text) as published by Harvard University Press, brought out by the Murthy Classical Library of India, Volumes 1 to 8 (London, 2015, 2016, 2017, 2018, 2019, 2020, 2021 and 2022 respectively). I have also consulted the Persian edition of *Ain-i-Akbari* (Aligarh, 2005) by Syed Ahmed Khan. I consulted

Three Memoirs of Homayun (California, 2009) translated by Wheeler M. Thackston that includes books commissioned by Emperor Akbar to help Abul Fazl write the *Akbarnama*. I found Mansura Haidar's *Mukatabat-i-Allami* (New Delhi, 1998) useful for details of Akbar's correspondence—as drafted by Abul Fazl—with various contemporary rulers and his nobles. There are other official accounts that would fall in the same category: Tasneem Ahmad's translation of *Tarikh-i-Akbari* (Delhi, 1993); the original Persian text of *Tarikh-i-Akbari* edited by Haji Muinuddin Nadwi, Azhar Ali Dihlawi and Imtiaz Ali Arshi (Rampur, 1962); and Brajendranath De's translation, *The Tabaqat-i-Akbari of Khwajah Nizamuddin Ahmad*, Volumes 1, 2 and 3 (Kolkata, 2015). I have relied upon A.S. Beveridge's translation of the *Baburnama* (Delhi, 2012) as well as that of W.M. Thackston (New York, 2002). I also consulted Yugjeet Navalpuri's Hindi translation of the *Baburnama* (New Delhi, 1991). The English translation of the *Maathir-ul-Umara* (Kolkata, 2003), a compendium of biographies of officers of the medieval age, translated by Henry Beveridge and revised, annotated and completed by Baini Prashad, is useful for biographical and other details.

The second observation post is that of the orthodox Mullah Abdul Qadir Badayuni who saw the Emperor from close and wrote a secret account that was discovered after Akbar's death. Badayuni had his reasons to be miffed with Akbar and he does not mince his words. His bitter outpouring offers a viewpoint far different from that of the loyalist Abul Fazl. Quotes and information from Mullah Abdul Qadir Badayuni's *Muntakhab-ut-Tawarikh* are mostly derived from George S.A. Ranking's translation (New Delhi, 1990).

The third observation post is that of the Jesuits who had come to Akbar's court to convert him. They spent substantial time with Emperor Akbar, often in exclusive meetings. Theirs is an account whose merit lies in the fact that it was not written for Akbar. They freely recorded their observations and interactions as it was to meant to reach their superiors.

For the account of Jesuits, J.S. Hoyland and S.N. Banerjee's *The Commentary of Father Monserrate* (New Delhi, 2003) has been very useful. So was *Akbar and Jesuits* (Delhi, 2008) of Father Pierre Du Jarric. I also found John Correia-Afonso's *Letters from the Mughal Court* (Anand, 1980) useful for the letters of the Jesuit priests at Akbar's court. For the wheels within wheels of the Jesuit-Akbar interaction as also for information regarding trade and commerce, I have found Pius Malekandathil's *The Mughals, The Portuguese and the Indian Ocean* (Delhi, 2013) enlightening. From Pedro Moura Carvalho's *Mirat al-quds (Mirror of Holiness): A Life of Christ for Emperor Akbar* (Leiden, 2012), I have consulted the Persian original and the English translation by W.M. Thackston.

For a common man's perspective on Akbar, I read Rohini Chowdhury's translation of *Ardhkathanak* by Banarsidas (New Delhi, 2009).

Iqtidar Alam Khan's paper "Akbar's Personality Traits and World Outlook—A Critical Appraisal" in *Akbar and His India* (New Delhi, 2010), edited by Irfan Habib, has been especially useful for getting into the Emperor's mind; also helpful have been "Akbar and Technology" by Irfan Habib and "The Image of Akbar as a Patron of Music in Indo-Persian and Vernacular Sources" by Francoise 'Nalini' Delvoye from the same volume. Athar Ali's "The Vision in the Salt Range,

1578: An Interpretation" in his book *Mughal India* (New Delhi, 2006) has also been enlightening for an understanding of Akbar's state of mind and his strategies around the time he marched to Bhera (including the zigzag route he took). Iqtidar Alam Khan's works, *The Political Biography of a Mughal Noble: Munim Khan Khan-i Khanan* (New Delhi, 1991), *India's Polity in the Age of Akbar* (Ranikhet, 2016), and *The Mughal Nobility* (Ranikhet, 2016), Shireen Moosvi's *Episodes in the Life of Akbar* (New Delhi, 2010), H.M. Elliot and John Dowson's volume 5 and 6 of their *History of India, as Told by Its Own Historians* (Delhi, 2014), G.M. Wickens's translation of *Akhlaq-i-Nasiri* (New York, 2011), and the original Persian text of the *Akhlaq-i-Nasiri*, the Lucknow edition (1957), have been useful for information and translations. Jos Gommans' *Mughal Warfare* (London and New York, 2002) gives an estimate of the time Akbar spent travelling. Harbans Mukhia's *The Mughals* was helpful in clarifying many issues related to Mughal History. *The Mughal Empire* (New Delhi, 2013) by John F. Richards, Satish Chandra's *Medieval India*-Part Two (New Delhi, 2014) were useful for the big picture of Akbar's age. Munis Faruqi's book *Princes of the Mughal Empire* (Cambridge, 2015) was useful in explaining the dynamics of the battle of succession among the Mughal princes. Athar Ali's *The Apparatus of Empire* (Delhi, 1985) was helpful in mapping the career of prominent nobles. A. Azfar Moin's the *Millennial Sovereign* (Delhi, 2017) explains Akbar's ambition in the spiritual space.

For the role of music in Akbar's life I consulted Bonnie C. Wade's *Imaging Sound* (Chicago, 1998). For the linkage between Akbar's power struggle with Bairam Khan and the theme of a specific painting, where the Emperor is holding a cheetah's ears, I found Susan Strong's *Painting for the Mughal Emperor* (London, 2002) useful. The above two works and many others were helpful for giving a visual insight into Akbar's life. I can recall a few (though I am indebted to many more): B.N. Goswamy's *Painted Visions* (New Delhi, 1999); John Guy and Deborah Swallow's *Arts of India* (London, 2004); Rosemary Crill and Kapil Jariwala's *The Indian Portrait* (Ahmedabad, 2010); Milo Cleveland Beach's *The Imperial Image* (Ahmedabad, 2012); *Masters of Indian Painting* (2011), edited by Milo C. Beach, Eberhard Fischer and B.N. Goswamy; Som Pal Verma's *Painting the Mughal Experience* (New Delhi, 2005) and *Mughal Painters and their Work* (Delhi, 1994); Linda York Leach's *Mughal and Other Indian Paintings* (London, 1995); K.K. Aziz's *The Meaning of Islamic Art* (Lahore, 2004); Kalpana Desai's *Jewels on the Crescent* (Mumbai, 2002); Andrew Topsfield's *Indian Paintings* (Oxford, 1994); Nasser D. Khalili's *The Timeline History of Islamic Art and Architecture* (2005); Toby Falk and Mildred Archer's *Indian Miniatures in the India Office Library* (London, 1981); Barbara Schmitz and Ziaud-Din Desai's *Mughal and Persian Paintings and Illustrated Manuscripts in The Raza Library, Rampur* (New Delhi, 2006); B.N. Goswamy's *The Spirit of Indian Painting* (New Delhi, 2014) and *Indian Costumes in the Collection of the Calico Museum of Textiles* (Ahmedabad, 2010); Asok Kumar Das's *Wonders of Nature: Ustad Mansur at the Mughal Court* (Mumbai, 2012); B.N. Goswamy's *Patkas in the collection of the Calico Museum of Textiles* (Ahmedabad, 2008); Usha R. Bala Krishnan and Meera Sushil Kumar's *Dance of the Peacock* (Mumbai, 1999); Daniel Walker's *Flowers Underfoot* (London, 1998); Amina Okada's *Indian Miniatures of the Mughal Court*

(New York); Amin Jaffer's *Beyond Extravagance* (New York, 2013); and Eleanor Sims's *Peerless Images* (Ahmedabad, 2002).

Since Akbar has been a part of me since the early years of my life, it would be difficult to recall and mention all the books and sources that went into the making of this book. However, I have mentioned a few that I have consulted in recent times. They can be consulted should a person want to go into greater details of the Emperor's work and life. I crave the indulgence of those authors whose contribution in shaping my understanding of Akbar over a lifetime goes unacknowledged.

Acknowledgements

As always my deepest gratitude to Naved Masood Saheb for going through the text and suggesting corrections and improvements. I am grateful to Ravi Singh of Speaking Tiger who immediately accepted the idea when I first broached it, and to Tahira Thapar and Nazeef Mollah for their diligence in making it a better book. My gratitude to my friend Rishi Sinha for his constant help.

Thank you Rumana, Kabeer, Tara and Arzoo you for your presence in my life.